A Wing in the Door

Also by Peri Phillips McQuay

The View from Foley Mountain

A Wing in the Door

Life with a Red-Tailed Hawk

Peri Phillips McQuay

MILKWEED EDITIONS

Published 2001 by Milkweed Editions
Printed in Canada
Cover and interior design by Dale Cooney
Cover painting by Fran Gregory
Author photo by Barry McQuay
Cover and interior photos of Merak courtesy of the author
The text of this book is set in Sabon.
01 02 03 04 05   5 4 3 2 1
First Edition

Milkweed Editions, a nonprofit publisher, gratefully acknowledges support from our World As Home funders: Lila Wallace-Reader's Digest Fund and Reader's Legacy underwriter Elly Sturgis. Other support has been provided by the Elmer L. and Eleanor J. Andersen Foundation; James Ford Bell Foundation; Bush Foundation; General Mills Foundation; Honeywell Foundation; Jerome Foundation; McKnight Foundation; Minnesota State Arts Board through an appropriation by the Minnesota State Legislature; Norwest Foundation on behalf of Norwest Bank Minnesota; Lawrence and Elizabeth Ann O'Shaughnessy Charitable Income Trust in honor of Lawrence M. O'Shaughnessy; Oswald Family Foundation; Ritz Foundation on behalf of Mr. and Mrs. E. J. Phelps Jr.; John and Beverly Rollwagen Fund of the Minneapolis Foundation; St. Paul Companies, Inc.; Star Tribune Foundation; Target Foundation on behalf of Dayton's, Mervyn's California, and Target Stores; U.S. Bancorp Piper Jaffray Foundation on behalf of U.S. Bancorp Piper Jaffray; and generous individuals.

Library of Congress Cataloging-in-Publication Data

McQuay, Peri Phillips, 1945–
    A wing in the door : life with a red-tailed hawk / Peri Phillips McQuay.— 1st ed.
      p.   cm.
    ISBN 1-57131-239-0 (hc.)
    1. Red-tailed hawk—Ontario—Anecdotes.   2. McQuay, Peri Phillips, 1945– I. Title.
    QL696.F32 M38 2001
    598.9'44—dc21

                                                        00-060091

This book is printed on acid-free, recycled paper.

For Morgan, Jeremy, and Merak,
with love.

A Wing in the Door

A Note to Readers

At the risk of being accused of anthropomorphism, I am not going to apologize for using the pronoun "who," instead of "which," when referring to Merak and the other animal characters of this story. Nor will I try to excuse my humanizing interpretation of them. To me, existence begins with seeing plants and animals and people in an equalizing light of respect. It will not hurt any of us to make these connections for the space of a book.

Merak

A canticle of sun and wind
in bare branches,
and clear, forever-seeing air
of glistening pines
and fields of rime
and you, replete
and swaying
in every feather
to wind's song.

Photo Album

above: Merak searching for nest twigs in spring.

above: Merak vents her spleen on a flowerpot.

left: Merak tests my newly made willow garden trellis.

right: Barry gets help with
the garden from Merak.

below: Merak in flight,
killer talons outstretched.

left: Immature Merak,
still displaying barred
tail feathers.

below: On a motorcycle
that Jeremy salvaged from
the dump.

above: Merak's early spring
bath in a wheelbarrow.

right: Jeremy with his
special friend.

above: Merak displaying
fine new tail feathers, some
not yet full length.

left: Merak's sense of play.

above: Wings and wheels—Merak taking flight from Jeremy's motorcycle.

above: Merak adjusting an egg on her first, ill-chosen nest outside the front door on our front porch.

above: Merak exploring her new home soon after her release.

A Wing in the Door

Prologue

All my girlhood, without ever knowing it,
I was dreaming wildness.

I grew up in a small woods and, because of my parents' solitary
life, the trees became more my kin than people ever will be. Alas,
for all its charm, my woods was threatened on all sides by exploitation. Looking out from the profound shade of lacy hem-
locks, I saw a world bereft of trees and found no place for myself
there, although I could not have said so then. Where I did belong,
what my heart cried out for, I was unable to envision. Except
that once there was one beaver pond.

My uncle, who delights in wildness, has worked faithfully to
preserve it. When I was thirteen, Joe told my parents about a
property his outdoors club was buying to turn into a conservation area. He tried to say how much it meant to him. He told us
we should go and have a look at it sometime. Yet when I did go
with my family, I found the resounding solitude and the unending
possibilities at first boring and then frightening. My artist parents, eyes searching for scenes, explored briefly, and then set up
their easels to paint. "Why don't you go for a walk," they suggested absently.

To stand still and contemplate the silence and the strangeness was unthinkable. Wholly ill at ease, I wandered off alone across sparse fields sprouting with scrub, drawn toward a distant forest by water music. Soon after, I entered a nightmare, becoming lost as I never had been before. Barely had I slipped inside this utterly foreign, seemingly endless woods, than the silence was reeling in my head; the silver-trunked trees were staggering dizzyingly about me. Never had I even dreamed of being so lost. At my feet was a tiny pool, a dew-pond of a pool. As I looked at it in my whirling, the leaves reflected in its bottom grew corpselike, leering, shivering. The leaves and the shimmering trunks seemed to be hissing that I could go on in this dreadful place forever and be nothing. I could be lost forever and no one would find me. Simply by entering this wildly echoing, empty land, I would cease to be.

Fleeing this lostness, I stumbled on, clinging to the sound of water that had drawn me to the forest. I plunged wildly up a bank, snatching at trunks to help me, and came out upon the broad expanse of the first beaver pond I had ever seen. Too exhausted by my terror to continue, I sank down on a fallen trunk, my breath shuddering.

The stillness was intense, but no longer menacing. A pair of harlequin-colored wood ducks sailed near the far edge of the pond. Closer by, rings burst on the mirror surface of the pond, and a V-shaped wake streamed across the water. While I crouched, the V drew gently closer, until I could detect a slick wet head with dark eyes studying me, waiting for me to state my place in his scheme of things. Surrounding me now were no longer the waves of my terror—instead there was the purl of water in a trickling fall from the nearby beaver dam. A slight breeze riffled the pond's surface and subsided. I leaned forward to see the beaver more closely, but that brought a resonant, reproachful thwack, and the animal sank out of sight. Fear completely forgotten, I crept to the edge of the pond, hidden among the rustling grasses, and simply waited to see what would happen next. Clouds scudded across the water; sinewy schools of minnows threaded their way amid the reeds beneath the surface. On a floating log, armored turtles shone in the heavy sun. Never had I felt such a complete connection with place.

But before the beaver surfaced again, my father's cheery whistle sounded, and he stepped into the clearing, come to fetch me now that his painting was done. Although I went willingly, obedient to my memory of the danger of being lost, in a way, I never left. I never would be able to leave the idea of the pond, the ducks, the beaver, more highly colored, more real than anything else I had ever encountered.

A tumult of school and university, marriage and children, followed. The memory of the beaver pond lay submerged deep within me, waiting.

For eight years my husband, Barry, and I and our two small sons, Morgan and Jeremy, kept moving, seeking jobs that would bring us closer to our heart's desire, a home in a rural area. We stood with small Morgan in a shower of wild geese at Jack Miner's sanctuary, and I wanted to never leave. A day later, returning into the city through the wasteland of suburbs, I thought I was suffocating, and this claustrophobia remained with me as long as I lived in the city.

In time we were able to move to a generous farmland. On autumn afternoons, I walked baby Jeremy across pastures to a tiny glade, where I held him up to pet the trees. But still a part of me knew I needed more. One day, casually, I asked my friend Pat McManus where I could find first-growth forest to visit, and he told me of a wild conservation area he knew of. He also mentioned, in an offhand way, that there might be a job as supervisor and teacher of conservation education available there in a year.

It seemed inconceivable to leave the security of Barry's well-paid teaching job and the pleasant farm area. "Why lad, you're too young to retire," an old farmer friend said in disgust when Barry told him what we were considering. Neither of us knew what it would really mean to disappear into such an isolated place. Still, on New Year's Eve, 1974, with a carload of children, cats, dog, books, and plants, I followed Barry and his truck to our new home.

In the sanctuary of the conservation area's eight hundred acres of forests, ponds, and derelict fields, I began exploring my childhood dream. For fourteen years I walked the fields, scrambled over rock faces, fingered lichen, watched the lives of deer. But always as an outsider. It was only with the coming of Merak, the human-imprinted red-tailed hawk, that I was challenged to confront the truths of wild living in a way that I could never have predicted.

From the first time I saw deer moving like shadows across a frozen beaver pond, from the first time I walked for miles to climb up on the granite ridges and gazed for great distances across snowy vistas, from the first time I stood shrouded in pines, listening to the soughing spring wind, I was surprised by the grace of finding myself moving so surely toward wildness. I knew, without the least doubt, that I was home at last. But only by living the realities could I earn my own place in this wildness. No dream could be as rich, nor as demanding. I was to find that both the terror and the bliss that I had experienced that long-ago day at the beaver pond were part of what I must learn.

When she came to us, like me, Merak was teetering on the edge of being wild but had much to learn before she would be able to live freely. Sharing her uncertainties and her difficulties would surely help me to understand.

Merak's Story

—Aug. 5, 1987 Red-tailed Hawk 1000 g seized by Ministry of Natural Resources in Kingston area from man trying to raise for falconry. Beautifully cared for, can hunt, sweetly tame and very responsive to humans. In flying trim—could fatten up. Here to untame. Transferred to Maberly in December.
—NOTE FROM KIT CHUBB'S AVIAN CARE AND RESEARCH FOUNDATION RECORDS

On a bright, windy day in late April 1988, six of us are walking over the winter-bleached grass to the field behind our barn. We are following a seventh, who is carrying a large box. The previous night, Kit Chubb, of the Avian Care Foundation, had phoned Barry and me with a request.

Earlier that spring Kit had used our conservation area home as a safe release spot for a bewitching pair of newly rehabilitated short-eared owls. Gently, we had opened their rustling box and tipped the small birds into our garden. Then we had watched as they sat for more than an hour getting their bearings. Their intense owlishness, and the beautiful gray, black, and silver mottling of their feathers had been captivating. Apparently fearless, but more likely shocked by their release into completely unfamiliar territory, their only motion had been the swivelling of their

heads, which enabled their eyes to reconnoiter their foreign surroundings. As soon as dusk had fallen, the charming pair had
swiftly disappeared, heading for the distant oak woods, and had
never been seen nor heard from by us again. Which was just as
Kit had hoped it would be.

This time, with a slight hesitation in her voice, which should
have prepared me, she had asked if we would be willing to accept
for release an immature, two-year-old female red-tailed hawk. She
had explained that the hawk had been taken from the nest as a
baby by a would-be falconer. Although the captor apparently had
treated the chick well, it is against provincial law to hold wild
creatures captive, so a representative from the Ministry of Natural
Resources had removed the young, partially trained hawk and
had given her to the Avian Care Foundation to be checked and
released. Because this had happened late in the previous season,
it was unlikely that the hawk would have been able to establish
a territory successfully at that time, so Kit had placed the bird
in a volunteer's aviary to overwinter and become untame.

This morning, seven of us are crossing the field: Kit and her
husband, Robin; John, the hawk's winter keeper; our thirteen-
year-old son Jeremy; Jeremy's friend Nathan; and Barry and I.
John tells us how he had carefully restricted his contact with the
hawk so it would be prepared to return to the wild. Nevertheless,
the as-yet-unseen bird is talking sweetly from within the box with
a quality of voice I have never heard before from a fierce bird of
prey. And I find myself wondering how tame the hawk might be.
"She should just go wild again," Kit had said on the phone the
night before. "I'm sure she can hunt for herself and she should do
fine. Probably it will be as it was with the owls; we'll just let her
go and you'll never see her again."

"But," she added thoughtfully, "she may well make her

territory near you. You should keep a lookout. She may find a mate and nest nearby."

This morning, however, Kit is a little doubtful. "You never know. She *might* be human imprinted. The falconer might have taken her from the nest too early, causing her to identify with humans, not hawks. It's pretty hard to tell. It could be that some day you'll find her swooping down to help you in your garden. You wouldn't mind that, would you?"

Mind! Although I had had no previous experience caring for even small birds, let alone a large hawk, the thought of living closely with this wild creature is exhilarating. We might be falconers, gaily striding through the field in the freshening breeze, preparing for a morning's sport. Instead, in the language of falconers, we are hoping to "hack" this red-tail: return her to complete liberty. As we walk, we are agreeing on how important it is for the hawk to have a chance of living a wild life, to be free of human contact. And yet a lurking something makes me half wish that the young hawk would at least remain nearby. I have never known a bird intimately.

Considering further, Kit offers reflectively, "Human-imprinted hawks can be an awful nuisance. They're so babyish and insistent. I hope you won't mind if . . . but I really don't think she *is* human imprinted. . . ." Mostly, though, we all talk with assurance about how fine it will be to return this hawk to wildness. Meanwhile, as we approach our designated release point, from within the box there is a flouncing of feathers.

When we tip her out of the box and into the field, I can see from the way the young hawk watches John that, in spite of his good intentions, she feels intimately toward him. Without appearing to watch, she knows where he is at every moment. Her infantile chatter to him pronounces that all is well so long as he is there. This is our first familiarity with her, and is supposed to be the last. We surround her in the long, dead grass, seeing a fierce eye and rapier talons, but hearing the soft talk.

At last, after twenty minutes of our admiration, John is impatient to see how she will do, and he nudges her with a piece of straw. Awkwardly, the great bird beats off across the field to the tall cottonwood trees in front of our house. But as she brushes past me, the powerful sweep of her wings rowing the air brings me to tears. In this brief passage I understand that the air is richer for her presence.

Safe in the trees, she practices teetering hops from branch to branch, as would a child hopping on and off a step. There is a sober elation to her accomplishments. She seems to be holding up her feathers like a little girl hampered by long skirts.

Between hops she is looking and looking, searching the winds and a vastness of sky we never can imagine. On this first day, as I watch her, she becomes "Merak," a word of Arabian derivation, which is also the name for the second bowl star of the Big Dipper. The Arabian meaning of "Al Marakk," the original of "Merak," is "loin of the bear," a fitting name for this savage predator who yet will let us see her intimate, tender side.

When she arrived, Kit gave us a bag of frozen mice to get us started. While we are waiting to see what the hawk will do next, and at John's suggestion, we build a feeding platform. We find a place back in the field, away from people and pets, where food can be laid out for the hawk if she should be slow in starting to hunt for herself. After we finish the platform, realizing that it will take time for the hawk to become oriented to her new surroundings, Kit, Robin, and John leave.

For the next two hours Barry and the boys and I watch the hawk through the bare branches of her tree. Never having seen a red-tail closer than a distant tree or soaring in the sky, I am amazed by the size of this buzzard. After Kit had phoned the previous night, I had looked up the hawk's measurements in a field guide: *"Buteo jamaicensis:* length 45–55 cm and wingspread 110–132 cm."

But only at the kind of close range we now have can I appreciate what a very grand bird this is. Because she is only two years old, her coloring and silhouette differ from what they will be when she matures this summer. Her tail is longer than it will be later this year, and her body is longer in proportion to her width. Most noticeable is that she has yet to develop the mature hawk's splendid rufous tail; hers is light brown, with narrow dark bands of equal width.

Eventually, convinced that she is there for the afternoon, Barry and I leave for a walk, charging Jeremy and Nathan to keep an eye on her. But when we return an hour later, the hawk is gone. Jeremy reports that they had watched her swoop down to the field and catch a mouse. He says she let them approach and watch her eat it, talking to them sideways out of her beak. Then she had flown off, leaving the tree exceedingly empty. Apparently the release has been successful; Merak is independent.

She does not return for a week, long enough that I abandon my dreams of having a hawk for a gardening companion. When we do see a hawk, it is flying so high that we can't identify it. Then, surprisingly, on May 4, I see one banded hawk hovering low over our house, followed by the usual resident pair that inhabit the fields beyond the distant treeline behind the house. It is uncommon for hawks to fly together in spring, but all three dip and swoop in amity around our fields. I am astonished by my joy at seeing her again.

Two days later, Barry sees the hawk, on her own once more,

calling uncertainly in woods. This is the week that Evan, Barry's summer biology student assistant, has come to work at the park. While he is rehearsing flower identification on the wildflower trail, Evan is pulled up short by coming face-to-face with Merak, perched in a bush. He is taken aback by how familiar the wild bird is with him. He comes to get us, but she has vanished before he can show us where she was.

Then two weeks of silence follow. Well, we have seen enough to believe she can fend for herself, and we know that hawks and owls do come and go from our area, depending on the supply of mice. Moreover, we know from our own experience with empty mousetraps that mice have been in short supply this spring. It is likely that she has moved on to better hunting grounds.

Almost a month after Merak's release, Ruth, a birdwatcher and conservationist who lives in the village nestled just beneath the ridge of our park, phones Barry to complain of a nuisance red-tailed hawk. It is banded, she tells him, and so tame it has approached people and even has hectored cats through screen doors. People are afraid for their children, she says, and there is even talk of one of the fathers doing the bird in with a baseball bat. Knowing exactly to which hawk Ruth is referring, Barry rounds up Evan for backup and hastens into town. Just as Ruth had described it, he finds the hawk crouching beneath a porch. Wary of gleaming eye, savage beak, and talons, Barry secures the wretched fowl's confidence with a mouse, and he and Evan swathe her in the indignity of a butterfly net and bring her back to the park in disgrace.

Once home, they cautiously untangle her and let her go at the feeding platform we built in the field on the day when she first had been released. While the rescue was taking place, I had hastily thawed a few mice from Kit's bag and laid them on the platform. Now Barry, Evan, and I stand by Merak while she eats, her wings draped and huddled over her sodden mice. Why has she become so desperately tame? What will she do now? What will we do if she returns to town? Kit had thought the park would be an ideal release point for her, being about two miles from the town. But it seems the hawk is prepared to go further afield. Perhaps tormenting the villagers amuses her. More likely, an urgent need for food has driven her to it. After her feed, the hawk flaps stolidly out of sight, leaving us with no answers.

All weekend she remains absent and once again we are worried for her. But on Monday, at first light, the shrieks we hear coming from the orioles nesting in our trees alert us. "That hawk's back," announces Morgan, when he rises half an hour later to get ready for school. Gingerly, Barry plucks several thawed mice from a bag in the refrigerator and dodges the hunger-crazed bird through the field to give her the sodden bodies at her feeding platform. After stuffing the mice into her crop, Merak flies to, and awkwardly scrambles up, the metal barn roof, with a sound reminiscent of fingernails scraping on a blackboard. Untroubled by her noisy, clumsy ascent, she perches like a Russian icon at the barn's front peak. It would appear that at last Merak has made up her mind that she will live with us.

Red-tails are one of the largest of our hawks and, as such, are slow to mature. Although the young can feed themselves at five weeks, birds of prey are dependent on their parents for several months after they have fledged. The parents do not teach the young; rather they lead them to fruitful hunting sites, where the fledglings must learn by experience. Considerable skill is needed to catch food. Even for adults, the failure rate of hunting is high.

Now, and over the next month, the great raptor shows us a piti-ful, urgent hunger for food and attention. I begin to wonder if she had caught much at all during her first month out of captivity. Since her return to us, we have only seen her catch a dragonfly.

And there is a new worry: A few days after Merak's return, Kit calls to tell me that someone from Westport has reported that a "crazed hawk" bashed into a house at the foot of the ridge, and then for two hours had been too stunned to leave. Surely that hawk is Merak. Could she have sustained brain damage? What will we do if she has?

If Merak is to live with us, I will need to understand as much as I can about the ways of hawks and the difficulties of this particular one. The first books I can locate are those written by falconers. Falconers have a long history of exceptional partnerships with their birds, and a wealth of lore from that experience. For at least four thousand years, falcons and other birds of prey have been used in hunting, first in Asia, then in Persia, and then, by A.D. 600–800, in central Europe. In the fifteenth and sixteenth centuries, monarchs had falconers in their courts and kept stables of birds, which they used for sport.

While highly unhelpful, early manuals of falconry prove fasci-nating to read. For example: to fly a goshawk, one advises,

> at the hour of vespers hold her on your fist until you go
> to bed; then put her on her perch, covered . . . and put a
> lighted candle in a lamp before her and leave it there all
> night. At daybreak, sprinkle her with wine and dry her be-
> fore a bright and smokeless fire. When it is light, fly her.

From these, I turn to more recent works.

Many modern falconers believe that a "passager" red-tail (one that is captured at less than a year old but independent) is ideal for their sport. The difficulty is that passager birds are more challenging because of their inherited wildness. For instance, they are much more likely to soar when they are released after prey, so the risk of losing such a bird is greater. Since Merak's captor was almost certainly a novice, he may have believed that training an eyas, or nestling, would be easier because of its tameness. Moreover, I learn from author Frank Beebe that, since the 1960s, red-tails like Merak, unfamiliar to medieval falconers, have become the most widely used in North America. The species is common, easy to obtain, and has a steady, even temperament that makes it easy to train.

⁓

Meanwhile, for all our worries about her future, we are experiencing an extraordinary intimacy with a magnificent wild bird.

All too quickly, there comes an afternoon when Barry has to be away and I am confronted with having to make, on my own, the long, vulnerable walk across the open field to give Merak her mice. And I have no way of knowing whether the unpredictable young female will accept me as a substitute for Barry. I am mindful of thirteenth-century King Dancus of Armenia, who cautioned:

> When she is angry or enraged, the falconer must be patient and treat her gently. Sometimes when her quarry escapes she becomes so enraged that she attacks her falconer and strikes his face or his horse's head, or sometimes one of his dogs. A good falconer must be patient and hide his anger, taking care not to call the falcon until her anger has calmed down.

Uncomforted by the high, clear light of a late afternoon in June, or the wind sweeping the grasses around my knees, I proceed warily, hoping with an improbable hope to reach the feeding platform before Merak notices what I am about. Alas, all too quickly I am assaulted by the infantile bird's hungry screams, and I see her lunging, rather than flying, toward me. Until this horrifying moment, when I come face-to-face with them, I have not appreciated just what devastatingly effective weapons her rapier talons are. Worst of all, in past encounters the hawk has shown herself to be wildly temperamental and unpredictable. Shall I drop to the ground, covering my face? At the last heart-stopping moment, she veers aside and strikes out for the platform, where she makes a heavy landing. She screams lustily as I approach, and the screams escalate as, with a shaking hand, I pitch the soggy, gray mouse bodies onto the platform in front of her. Pinning them with her talons, she pivots so that her back is to me, flares her tail, and shrouds the platform with her outspread wings. (Later I will learn that falconers call this defensive sheltering of prey "mantling.")

Shaken by the difficult passage to the feeder, I stand by her while she gulps her mice. My reward for the harrowing trip across the field is stroking her after she has finished. I know all there is to know about the favorite stroking spots of cats and dogs, but nothing about how one should approach a hawk. Warily, I stretch out my hand to the top of her small head. I can cup it in the curve of my hand. Then I mantle the hawk with both my hands, just as she mantled her food. Like a camera shutter, her milky, bluish third eyelid shoots across to protect her startled eye. Where proper eyelids are closed only in sleep, the third, or "nictitating eyelid," removes dirt and spreads tears but, because it is transparent, doesn't impair vision.

But today Merak merely allows, rather than relishes my petting. Standing there with the wind rushing around us, I take in the pattern of her feathers—dapples, stipples, "eyes" like those on peacock plumage. I discover that there are slight whiskers around her beak. I examine her yellow legs, which medieval kings described as "covered with scales like those on a snake's belly," and her eyes "bright as a flame." Then, without warning, and with a parrotlike squawk, the red-tail launches herself off the platform, flapping raggedly across the field toward the west-lying oak woods.

I begin to appreciate the hollowness of an airborne creature, which begins with many hollow bones, but even more so consists of a curving of feathers and rounded body, all of which buoy air inward, stirring it to her center, as if she herself were only slightly more than air. Now I know that the hawk looks large, but in reality is little more than the sum of her feathers, held together by an indelible personality.

Standing beside the feeding hawk, I was amazed by the swivel of her head. Even over the course of the twenty minutes she stayed with me, she displayed a vast variety of positions, each changing her aspect substantially. Indeed, she is immensely faceted. I am beginning to see that the combination of wildness and domestication results in an overlay that makes her highly complex. Where I might say ten or fifteen things in description of a cat or dog, I could easily find fifty for her.

⌒

Over the next few weeks we begin to discover the costs of having a half-wild hawk close to home. Although alive to the irony of cats being preyed on by a bird, the situation that now confronts us (and our four cats) is no joke. We remember the savage jealousy of the domesticated wild otters in Gavin Maxwell's *Ring of Bright Water* with concern, and each day it is becoming clearer that our difficult bird now regards us as her exclusive property. It would be the work of a moment for the hawk to slash to death one of the pets we love and protect, as we nearly witness when

Kitty, the little black kitten, while sheltered by a flowerpot, engages in a furious and futile boxing match on the back porch with the bird, and then decides that his joyous days of going out are over.

Our resident wildlife is also disturbed by the ever-present hawk. It is now the peak of nesting season, when birds are at their most territorial, and the wild birds are distressed by the presence of what they believe to be a dangerous predator. Sadly, the orioles that have nested in our cottonwoods ever since we came to the conservation area have been driven off; after a week of seeing dazzling orange flashes dart about in distress, we find they have abandoned their beautiful hanging silken nest. One morning we actually see Bird racketing around the barn with an indignant phoebe perched on her back. (I have taken to calling the hawk *Bird* because right from the beginning she has seemed to me the quintessential bird. In other words, she is not just any bird; she is *every* bird.)

Every day we are wrenched from sleep at dawn by a cacophony of indignant birds "telling" on Merak. Our female hairy woodpecker, who usually retreats deep into the woods in summer, returns to perform some irritable drumming and shrieking in her cottonwoods. Meanwhile, Merak sits, bewildered but not aggressive, while birds actually perch beside her on her barn roof, scolding frantically. At first the birds' racket is almost intolerable. Later many of them recognize that she is not a threat and largely accept her. Robins and then phoebes and wrens creep in to take the beautiful orioles' place. Still, we always know when Merak is near because of the protests of other birds, and so, since our resident hawk arrives to perch over our bedroom roof at the earliest light, sleeping in has become a thing of the past.

I am uncertain of how much food a free-living, but generally non-hunting, adult red-tail requires. Experts on feeding birds in captivity cannot know how much such a hawk should be fed. I increase her food to ten small mice a day and establish two firm feedings, one in the morning and one at teatime, hoping she will be more manageable. Otherwise, ever hopeful for handouts, she besieges anyone approaching or leaving the house.

Gradually, we become aware of an array of "displays": begging displays, such as those employed by chicks to solicit food, or by some females to solicit courtship feeding; greeting displays, when one parent relieves the other at the nest; and the all-too-frequent threatening displays.

We can no longer hope that this hawk, this curious assortment of avian and human qualities, is not human imprinted. She was taken too soon from the nest, and it is painfully apparent that she doesn't know how to be a proper hawk. She identifies with people rather than her own kind and, because she was separated from her parents too early, she has retained the worst of infantile characteristics and seems highly unpredictable.

Reading modern falconers on hawks captured as eyases (or babies) is not encouraging. I learn that an eyas becomes so tame and fearless that it eventually grows possessive, whereas a wild-caught passager bird retains a measure of respect for its captor. It may be that eyases do not have passager birds' assurance in hunting. While I discover from Frank Beebe that many "screamers" become less vocal with maturity, it may be that an eyas that has been kept as a pet, flown sporadically or not at all, and that has never hunted or killed, will continue to be infantile, possibly forever. Merak?

Apparently, adults don't train their young to hunt. Even captive birds can learn how to hunt without a teacher. However, unlike ducklings, which take to water within hours after hatching, hawks are among those birds that require a long period of parental supervision before they become independent. Young birds remain in the nest or nest tree for six to seven weeks. Even after they have left the tree they may return to roost in the nest for several days, and even after they are fledged they continue to associate with the family group for two months or more after first flight. It appears to be at this stage of hovering about us, her "family," that two-year-old Merak is presently stuck.

In fact, now that we are recognizing that she is likely to become a part of our lives, at least until we can help her return to living independently, we are beginning to find that wonderful Merak is becoming rather a pest. We always have to be wary when we go outside the door for fear she will pounce, doing no harm but flapping and squawking, insistent on food and attention. Merak has begun sitting on the two front porch railings, hopping from one to the other to get the best vantage point for watching us and wheedling us to come out—or rather, I fear, to let her come in. In fact, several times she actually has tried to shoulder her way in the door. The result of her choice of locations is that the front porch stoop generally, and most inconveniently, is splotched with large white droppings.

Her terrorism directed at the other occupants of our house has reached new lengths. On choice spring days the four cats, now housebound, like to sit sunbathing and savoring the breezes coming through the screened windows. Noticing the hawk perched in a nearby tree, but confident that the house is his sanctuary, Valentine, the elderly brown Siamese, sits in our bedroom window swearing boldly at her. Furious at the sight of this invader in her house, and ignorant of screens, Merak swoops directly at the cat. Inevitably, her talons snag in the mesh and my first worry is that she will be trapped in the screen, and that, in her desperation, she will be too dangerous for me to rescue. Instead, she wrenches her claws out, at considerable cost to the screen. Unfortunately, though, the war proves so appealing to all parties that the cats start teasing the hawk regularly through the window and she apparently relishes the entertainment. It is beginning to appear that replacing screens will become yet another regular necessity. And the feuding is not confined to cats. Wary at first with Annie and Savannah, our two older Cardigan Welsh corgis, Merak takes delight, in classic bully form, in blitzing Rosie, the puppy. Like the cats, Rosie is becoming more and more reluctant to leave the house.

If we are to live together, our challenge will be to teach the difficult red-tail to accept our ways and to tolerate our family of animals. But we can see that getting her to allow cats within *her* territory will be the scariest introduction we've ever had to make. She has demonstrated repeatedly that, in one of her highly unpredictable moods, she easily could destroy a cat. Indeed, her sinister claws and beak and occasionally exceedingly cold eye remind us that we ourselves (and our human visitors) might be at risk.

I am still asking myself how much we should and can intervene with this seemingly wild creature. Seeing that she has adopted our home as her territory and us as her fellow hawks, it is tempting to try to master some of the falconer's commands. Possibly the discipline, as in obedience training for dogs, would make her more willing to cooperate, and would give her a clearer understanding of what is expected of her. And yet our first goal, what we had promised Kit and John, and what we want ourselves, is to insure that Merak returns to the wild. With no experience, we only know that we are going to have to find a balance we can live with, while we try to help the hawk "untame" (as Kit calls it). As an Anglo-Norman treatise on falconry advised: "It is much better to take care, / To walk gently with small steps."

One summery evening we are sitting under the whispering cotton-woods, with Merak crooning drowsily overhead. "Well," Barry remarks, "we survived with Miss Fanny, and we learned a lot too. This new creature will be the same." The first wild creature who had lived with us and had taught us about wildness, Miss Fanny was an orphan skunk whose story I told in *The View from Foley Mountain*. As a baby, Fanny had been found lingering beside her dead mother by the side of the road. She had been descented and adopted by a farm boy, who had made a pet of her for a summer and then left her alone in his barn. Bereft of scent glands, the skunk would have been unable to defend herself, so we took her on. Barry had hoped to show her to schoolchildren visiting our park, but the traumas of her past life had made her so suspicious that it took Barry half a year and many needle-sharp bite wounds on his hands to win her confidence. Formidably shy, she never became tame enough to bear visitors, let alone classes of students, but she warmed to us, bustling about the house, thieving for her nest, hissing and stamping the human and animal population into submission.

"Do you remember the Ladies' Sewing Circle?" I asked Barry. When I was sitting by myself on the couch sewing, Fanny would haul herself heavily up the couch cover until she was beside me. After she had pulled up her drawbridge by tugging up the couch cover after her, she took a great interest in my work and "helped" by raking with her long, curved digging claws through my dish of pins, before draping her flat, striped body luxuriantly over my lap.

"Do you remember her nose?" Barry returns. Skunks are

nearly blind, but Fanny's quivering, pointed, chewing-gum-pink nose led her on her hustling dance about the floors of our house. So eloquent was her sniffing that it almost seemed to speak to us less-gifted humans.

"Don't forget how, when she was mad, she used to stamp and lurch forward so furiously she nearly fell over," added Morgan, on his way down to prowl on his favorite rocks.

Always recalcitrant, ever fascinating, the passionately loving and passionately independent skunk had shared our life for eight years, teaching us much about wild animals. In her old age, she softened, from wily and challenging to genial, no longer biting anyone—neither Kitty, who deserved it, nor aged cat Valentine, who did not. For her last year, she trundled leisurely about her scent routes of the house, spread herself on heat vents, and sought more love than ever. Gradually she slept longer into the nights, her active time. One evening in May she failed to haul herself up out of her skunk house at all, having sunk into a coma. Sorrowfully, because in old age only her best qualities had remained, Barry and I carried the small body out to the blossoming orchard and, among the birdsong and the flowers, Barry put a bullet cleanly in her small, wedge-shaped head. I wrapped her in a red cloth (red had always been her best color) and laid her in a grave with some of the flowers she had so relished sniffing. When we returned to the somehow quieter house, I mourned most that it was unlikely we ever would have such a rare experience again.

And yet, it was at the end of the week in which we lost Fanny that Merak was released in the park. Once again, and to a greater degree than before, we are to have the rare privilege of becoming acquainted with another relatively undomesticated creature.

In spite of the worries, there are golden moments with the

difficult hawk that more than compensate for all the problems she has brought with her. Deliberately, on her heels, she stalks the perimeter of the house, perching on the compost pail so she can peer in through our screened door; then she thoughtfully hops up the stairs one at a time to stand at the kitchen door, inviting Jeremy out to visit her. Merak has quickly elevated Jeremy to the role of special companion. My favorite picture is of him going out to keep the hawk company, sitting on a sunshiny, dandelion-starred lawn, and Merak happily settling beside him to sunbathe for the first time, flopping her wings out any old which way and kicking out her legs.

〜

I still am uncertain of how much, or even whether, to feed her. "Oh, she can hunt for herself, all right. I'm sure she can," Kit insists when I question her. "Look, it's summer, and there's lots of prey out there. You're spoiling her."

Yet Merak seems so desperate when I cut back her rations. In the first falconry manual I read there had been warnings about the dangers to health of both underfeeding and overfeeding a hawk. I remember her earlier raids in town and am afraid that the unpredictable Merak might return to begging there if she does not get fed by us. Moreover I am always mindful of farmers' distrust of hawks, and fearful that if she wanders off of our protected eight hundred acres and begins cruising over neighboring farms while still so tame, she might get shot.

My field guide lists the weight of a red-tail at between 1.5–3.3 pounds, so I have been trying various ruses to weigh her—trying to inveigle her onto bathroom scales with me, for instance—but I can't pretend to be achieving a useful reading. Just when I am becoming seriously worried about whether to supplement her food,

I read a second and more reassuring book, which suggests that red-tails and other buzzards actually can get by with surprisingly little food. Certainly, I have to think that when they exist in the wild their food sources must be unpredictable. It isn't until the end of June, when I actually watch her catch a chipmunk, that I begin to think that Kit is right, and that the hawk could manage very well on her own without handouts from us. Prowling on the front lawn, Merak hears a cheep from under the front porch and scuttles under the lattice. Her apparent disregard for the state of her feathers and even for her own safety never fails to astonish me. Since it seemed impossible that a hawk on foot could catch anything edible, I pay no more attention to her, and go on watering the flower beds at the side of the house. However, some minutes later, when I turn the hose to the herb garden sheltered in front of the porch, I hear proud talk and, peering under the porch, discover the hawk with a chipmunk secured within the round of her claws. After I go indoors, she takes it to the picnic table and guards it for an hour before she rips its head off and eats it.

My opinion about Merak, her abilities, and her relationship with us changes daily. She may be more independent than sometimes seems to be the case. I expected that she might sleep in our sheltering trees, even hoped she might roost on the flower box protected by the roof of our back porch, but from the beginning she plainly thought her sleeping was too private to share even with us. After hanging around until the last light is draining from the skies, she flaps off toward the dense protection of the pines at the distant edge of our surrounding fields. Her roosting spot and her private life when she is away from our house remain hidden from us until Barry, while leading a group of girl guides down the main road, catches her sleeping in a big pine beside the road.

She is beginning to molt her feathers, and I have been reading, trying to find out what to expect. Birds experience one complete molt each year, during which they produce a whole new set of feathers when the old, worn feathers are pushed out by new ones. The molt is timed to avoid the times of breeding and food short-age, and to produce the new feathers as an advantage in migra-tion. In the normal pattern of molt, the main flight feathers are shed in parallel sequence, on both sides of the body, so that bal-ance in flight is not impaired. Nevertheless, the sprouting feathers form gaps that must somewhat spoil the aerodynamic effect of the wings.

As we are to find with Merak, coincident with a red-tail's first molt is a gradual darkening of eyes, in which the irises will even-tually change to brown, and a yellowing of the exposed parts. One thing seems definite: "A molting hawk and a growing hawk," writes Jack Mavrogordato, "cannot be given too much food."

Is it that she trusts us enough now to let her hair—or, in this case, feathers—down? For she has been casting these about quite freely. Perhaps molting is as distressing and uncomfortable as teething. Whatever the explanation, she has been a devilish bird all day. She wouldn't come for her food until I left. Later I caught her picking up a fair-sized branch on the lawn and tossing it about like an irritable child. At noon I find that she has driven furious Small Cat behind a sheet of plywood on the back porch and is trying to dig her out when I intervene. (Small, the drag-onish old female Siamese and leader of our cat clan, had refused to be driven indoors by a mere bird.) Indeed, I am coming to sus-pect that the regular confrontations between cat and hawk are a source of perverse pleasure to both. I, however, remain haunted by uncertainty as to how far the hawk might go.

From my reading I can appreciate how characteristic her method of attack is, both with the chipmunk and with our cats.

Falconry expert Frank Beebe has observed that, unlike other raptors, rather than making surprise attacks from air, red-tails often position themselves between their prey and its shelter. In such situations, these hawks face the risk of having to stand their ground while they are savagely challenged by their victims.

Having dealt to her satisfaction with the cat, Merak struts around on her heels, plainly searching for something else annoying to do. (Incidentally, Small, whom I had pitied, is seething when I rescue her and immediately tries to go back out again.) The wily fowl hops on and off flower boxes, considering, as only birds do, and finally selects Jeremy's grandfather cactus. She drags the shaggy plant out of its pot and proceeds to shred it savagely, with superb disregard for its spines. When I remonstrate with her and remove the cactus with a wary foot, she stalks over and fetches a second plant, this one in a light plastic pot, and kicks it around the porch. I get that away too, and go indoors to await further wickedness. Luckily, at this point, a shower intervenes and she steps out onto an elm chopping block circle, where she fans and arches her wings into an avian umbrella, delighted and distracted by the rain. Yet all afternoon she's been lurking around the porch, and I can see in those expressive and contrary eyes of hers that she is only biding her time.

⁓

On a cool evening with tiny scatterings of rain interspersed with gleams of sun, Barry is thinning carrots in the vegetable garden while I am making a late sowing of seeds. With a scraping and scratching of claws, Merak thunks onto the barn roof, apparently curious to know what we are doing. And I am reminded of how, on the day of Merak's release, Kit had remarked, "Who knows, you might even find her helping you with your gardening." In spite of my sincere wish for her successful return to the wild, how I had wished that she would. Piqued by our work, she flies down to investigate what Barry is doing. She saunters through the plants, but fortunately, because she walks on her heels with her claws raised, they remain unharmed.

For a while she is content to "help" Barry by scratching the earth and earnestly cocking her head. When the thinning becomes boring, she does her scuttling rush over to investigate my work. By now I have moved on to transplanting seedlings sprung from seeds dropped by winter-feeding birds, and I explain to her that I am making the beginnings of a hawk jungle where only bare earth previously has existed. Truly pleased to see her in such an affable mood, I stroke her breast with a weed, and she sweetens her raucous talk and even caresses my hand with her beak.

Encouraged by her reception, she then actually picks up a seed packet in her beak and carries it over to Barry. Hardly knowing who is more in need of help, she then begins running back and forth between us. Soon the scene is interrupted when the screen door bangs and Jeremy approaches with a weed whacker, keeping his promise to cut the bushy fringe surrounding the vegetable garden. Cautiously, Merak mounts a tomato cage to keep an eye on him. On this night of uncommon tranquillity, I would say that she is superior to any cat or dog as a gardening companion. She has her own personality and interests, yet, when in high good humor, can be such a sociable, charming hawk.

June's last week, before the heat arrives in earnest, is filled with more pleasant pictures. One afternoon Merak makes Jeremy a nest out of a few haphazardly gathered sticks, snatches a dandelion from the lawn and presents it to him. Quite plainly, this is an invitation to set up housekeeping together.

Since the slightest breeze sets the leaves of the cottonwood in motion, many native tribes hold these trees in reverence, believing that they are specially sensitive to the presence of the Great Spirit. A few evenings after Merak's proposal to Jeremy, I hear the dooryard tree talking, with just the kind of modest, dusty sounds I imagine a tree would make. But then there is a rain of snowy belly feathers from out of the tree, and I know that the tree's voice is Merak's.

Often the hawk's speech is less pleasing. Red-tails are known to be a vocal species, easily annoyed or excited. And I am beginning to sense the breadth of Merak's vocabulary. Just as in the past I've found that other birds have a much wider range of speech than the official call given for each, Merak also has a great variety of sounds. Some are for rebuking, flirting, or commenting. Many are babyish. Unfortunately, so far she has made only a slight pretense at the magnificent keer of the adult. Even the tone of her responses to us is changing. When she is pleased with us, her mild haaawk has been tipping into a gull-like squeak at its end.

We still have a lot to learn about what our bird considers food. One day, Merak calls crossly to us from the chimney until her demands for food are appeased with two thawed rats. Wretchedly dissatisfied even after eating, she pretends she has never seen Barry before in her life and refuses to let him stroke her. The next day, with a buzzard's taste for carrion, while hanging around the picnic table she eats a star-nosed mole that one of the cats must have caught but rejected.

Meanwhile, the hawk-cat games continue, but appear to be less risky for the cats. One misty morning Merak, perched on the barn roof, gleefully points out Small to me, who is seeking refuge from the bird in the dense thicket of plum bushes behind the house. While the hawk does not actually go after her, that afternoon, as I head to the feeding station with the teatime ration of mice, the hawk actually bashes recklessly into the back of my knees in pursuit of the cat, who gamely but unwisely has been following me. With more composure than I myself can muster, Small stalks to midfield, where Merak scuttles at her, with more threat than intent. This oldest of our cats is then allowed to withdraw back to her plum bush refuge, with only the warning of a very light shrill cry from the bird.

Merak also begins to play games with us. When Jeremy practices archery, she stands by him and admires his shots. Barry offers her a stick for an arrow of her own and, entering wholeheartedly into the spirit, if not the sense, of the game, she kicks it and stamps on it gleefully, looking significantly at him as she does.

But the seesaw continues. July 1 is a day of high winds. In the morning Merak is reluctant to eat. Throughout the day I notice that her flying remains poor. She seems unpoised, probably because of the feathers she has shed. In the evening she flies to the barn, makes a poor landing (a phoebe has been clinging to her back), and skates back down the steep incline, ending miserably on a huddle of farm machinery on the far side of the barn. When she refuses to come to her feeding platform, I take pity and carry mice to her in the lee of the barn. Before she touches my offering I notice that there is a little dried blood on her beak and talons. Has she killed for herself this day?

For the next several days Merak refuses all food, and, foolishly, I worry about the overgrown infant hawk. Even though I know she is almost certainly molting, she appears so wretched and listless that I fear our magnificent bird has become ill, and I feel powerless to help her.

Always searching for suggestions for ways to understand and help Merak, I leaf through the Lewis Carroll-like realm of the early falconry manuals' remedies for ailing birds. Take, for instance, "The most frequent ailment of falcons is the headache. The symptoms of this trouble are present when the falcon closes her eyes and moves and turns her head in all directions." Briefly, I am susceptible to this suggestion. The present hot, humid weather is enough to give anyone a headache.

My faith is shaken, however, when I turn to a remedy for gout: "Take a snake called a tyrus, cut a handbreadth from the head and another from the tail end of the snake, and fry the middle part in a clean earthen pot; the grease which remains from the cooked snake should be given to the falcon, together with peacock meat, every day for eight days." Another suggestion has to do with voice: "If the goshawk is louder than she should be, feed her a bat, filled with ground pepper. On the other hand, if she peeps and seems to have lost her voice, pierce her nose with a brass needle."

By the following weekend the air is fiery by seven in the morning when Merak lands on our roof. I scuff through the dusty, bitter-scented dried grass of field to the feeding station, hoping against hope that this day the hawk will relent and that I will be able to tempt her to eat. On the way, through shimmering heat and grass, everywhere there are little s-curving rustles—of snakes winding, I imagine. But out of the great, sere emptiness of field and sky no bird comes to eat, and I must return alone to the house to wait. At suppertime I throw this morning's thawed mouse up to Merak, who, in the glaring late afternoon heat, is skulking on the porch roof. The mouse is declined.

In the evening, however, having moved to the shade of the cottonwoods, the hawk is taking more notice. I coax Jeremy to shinny up the tree with a rat for her. He crawls out on her limb and leaves it for her. She awks to us and wheeeeps to her mouse and accepts it from her safe, secluded perch. Deeply thankful that she has eaten, I lie for an hour in the chamomile-scented grass beneath the tree, just staring into her leafy bower and crooning to her.

A week later I am sitting out in the heavy, hot, humid evening trying to catch a breeze. Small wanders past. I call to her languidly but, busy about her own affairs, she ignores me. However, a few minutes later when Merak appears in the tree overhead, the cat immediately loses interest in the grasshopper she has been stalking and saunters over to me, deliberately making a show of claiming love. The bird, while observing her crossly, is clearly too uncomfortable to intervene. But when at last I rise to return to the house, the little Siamese follows me possessively, and Merak finds it worth her while to leave her tree and whoosh the arrogant cat. After that, with considerably less dignity, Small is persuaded to hustle into the house.

From the doorway I watch as Merak walks her ridiculous heel-to-toe shuffle over to the dogs' wading pool. I have not re-filled it for some days, but the hawk finds a puddle remaining in it, slakes her thirst, and proceeds to wet her belly. The prospect of the large, silly bird playing in the wading pool is irresistible, so I come out and add the contents of the nearby watering can and watch her having a lovely time pecking plastic and dipping her body into the pool. Comfortable at last, she walks back to the tree and makes a poor job of climbing it.

To be a molting bird must, I think, be like having to go back

each year to being a toddler after knowing what it's like to run
and leap.

～

While she is so awkward and uncomfortable she remains close to
the house and trees, and is easy to observe. In spite of our molting hawk's ill temper, we continue to get to know her better. One
afternoon, when Merak is hanging about the flower box on the
back porch, Jeremy strolls out to talk to her. Then, cautiously,
he extends his bare arm to her, offering it for a perch as a falconer might. She hesitates, and, not really knowing what he is
doing, he pushes his wrist back against the fronts of her yellow,
scaly legs. Promptly, the hawk ascends onto his wrist and lets
him carry her. She croons to him as they make a circle around the
house, and then he slips her off and back onto the flower box.

"What was it like?" I ask him. "What did it feel like?"

"Look at the marks she made, just hanging on." Jeremy points
to deep but unbroken dents in his skin.

"Is she heavy?"

"No, not at all."

But no description could substitute for experience. I cannot
imagine what it would be like to feel a hawk on my wrist, much
less to carry her perched there; so, before long I too extend my
wrist before her legs and coax the bird up on my arm.

What does it feel like? Well, the hawk's legs and feet are dry
and scaly, and feel rather like snakeskin, when she ascends. Once
she is securely roosted on my arm, I notice a surprising lightness
and featheriness. All the while that she clings to my wrist she is
tipping back and forth, righting herself and continually bringing
herself back to true. Through the touch of her flesh I can read
some of the sensations her constant vigilance brings her, as her

35

head swivels, responding. She reflects no alarm, nor panic, just a continual alert responsiveness to far more than I would ever be able to detect. Later Jeremy and I learn that carrying hawks can be risky without the heavy protective leather gauntlet that falconers use. But no matter what her mood, Merak will continue to be unfailingly gentle and secure on our wrists, and Jeremy and I never resort to a glove. This particular session ends with Merak "kissing" me intensely with her scimitar beak.

After this adventure, I wonder about the government's wisdom in seizing our hawk. It is indefensible to use wild birds for falconry. Moreover, it is clear that Merak's former captor had been unknowledgeable or he would not have removed her so early from her nest, leaving her infantile and apparently attached to humans for life. However, her willingness to come to our wrists and her frequent outbursts of affection suggest that a considerable bond must have formed between the would-be falconer and his hawk. Would Merak ever be happier than she was now, living open to the perils as well as the pleasures of freedom, yet babyish and seemingly unable to form a relationship with her own kind or fully support herself with her hunting? Even while recognizing the wrong done to her, I feel frequent flashes of regret for the broken attachment between the bird and her captor, and sorrow for the apparently equally imperfect world in which she now flies free.

What might Merak's life have been like if she had remained with her captor? For a good falconer, the relationship between human and hawk is one of partners, not master-servant. Falconers know that only with that kind of understanding and cooperation is "manning"—the process of the falcon becoming used to the falconer and his activities—possible. Our resident red-tail would have been used with certain classical equipment. She would have been fitted with jesses (leather straps, one for each leg), which are attached by swivels to a leather leash tied either to a leather glove worn by the falconer or to a moveable block or perch. She also would have had a leather hood, which would have fitted over her head to cut off light without interfering with her breathing or causing discomfort. Such a hood, simulating nighttime darkness, permits the bird to be carried without fright. Traditionally, both hood and jesses are supposed to be fashioned by the falconer.

Her training would have begun with a reduction of her weight to increase her need to hunt. At first she would have been encouraged to jump a few feet to the falconer's wrist for food, then she would have been flown to a lure (a light leather bag with food attached), which would have been tied at the end of an eight-foot cord. The lure would have been swung around the falconer's head to attract the hawk, and then allowed to fall to the ground, where she would have fed on it.

At first she would have been tied to a fifty-foot line called a creance in case she should try to fly away. Later, at the riskiest stage of training, she would have been allowed to fly free to the lure. If this first free flight had gone well, she would have been off the creance in a few days, and chasing game shortly thereafter.

⌒

For better or worse, however, Merak now is thoroughly part of our lives. A typical July day begins with her parading over the roof to Morgan's window at five in the morning and then walking fussily and noisily across the roof and out onto a roof-touching branch so that she can peer into our window. (When I arise, there is a downy little feather on the screen to prove it.) She then clanks her identification bracelet and gaaawks on the branch until we come and feed her.

Then comes a worrisome day when Merak is nowhere to be seen. Actually, by noon, I give up expecting her because it is blaringly hot, and it isn't until I hear robins fussing in the evening that I discover her. When she does show up I give her mice but am too uncomfortable myself to linger, and I figure she'll be irritable or indifferent anyhow. But she surprises me by seeming disappointed, expectant.

First thing next morning, she readily flies to the feeding station of her own accord. I take her three thawed mice, which she bolts into her crop, acting snappish until she is done stuffing. This gulping of food with little treatment means that she can gather large quantities in a short time. A bird saves food in her crop, a thin-walled bag that leads off the throat. Securing a large meal in a short time allows her to satisfy her hunger and to make the most of a source of food before competitors arrive. Time spent eating is time in which she is in danger. It is an advantage for her to be able to stuff the crop with food and return to the safety of trees or a "plucking post" pole. This storage also would help her collect food for young.

After she has had time to dissect her food in a more leisurely fashion with her beak, her food will be broken up in a two-chambered stomach. The anterior chamber secretes enzymes and hydrochloric acid, which start to break down the food. The posterior chamber, the gizzard, has a strong muscular wall which contracts rhythmically to grind the food. Eventually indigestible matter, such as bones and hair, will be ejected from the mouth as a pellet.

Standing by her, I feel rapt. It is that most primitive and absorbing first-baby feeling of being wholly engrossed. I pet her breast and she nips me, but with more politeness than conviction. We hear a mature red-tail in the back field, and Merak seems to shiver. A sadness sweeps over me that she has none of that other hawk's soaring, savage wildness. And for now, winter and next year's mating season remain mysteries. Meanwhile, I continue to find her bewitching, although I cannot fathom why I am so attached to her when she so often is such a peevish, difficult bird.

⁓

By the end of July a metamorphosis has taken place. There is no doubt that after a long and apparently uncomfortable molt, our hawk's formerly drab and tattered feathers are beginning to glow and her breast is coloring as it develops more reddish plumage than I had expected. We are excited to see that at long last new side tail feathers are coming in, which are the rich red of an adult red-tailed hawk. These two red, half-grown tail feathers are deepening in color every time I see her. Then a second rank of tail feathers begins to show, overlapping the first.

As I have seen, Merak literally *is* her feathers. They form a smooth, streamlined surface to the body and are raised, lowered, or rotated by muscles that attach to the walls of their sockets. Feathers perform several functions in addition to flight: they shield her from injury, sunburn, and rainfall, provide camouflage and insulation, promote displays, and line nests. To have feathers is to participate in a kind of continual resurrection, for, unlike the skin of bat wings, which tears easily, feathers can be sectionally replaced through molting. There are two general categories of feather: plumulae, or down (which nestlings also have), and penne, or outer feathers. These last are divided into contour feathers, covering the body, and flight feathers, providing a strong but light and flexible surface on the wings and tails. There are also specialized feathers such as the facial bristles I have enjoyed seeing. These last, like the whiskers of an animal, may augment a bird's sense of touch. All features are most wonderfully designed, each one constructed of closely set rows of filaments, called barbs, branching from a hollow rod. Each barb carries two rows of smaller filaments, the barbules, which must be kept hooked up. A bird such as Merak might have from fifteen hundred to three thousand feathers, which explains why preening (the careful cleaning, rearrangement, and oiling of the feathers with the bill) is such a constant chore for her. Preening arranges the barbs and removes dirt and parasites, except on her hard-to-reach head, which can only be scratched by foot.

During this preening, she transfers oil from the preen gland under the tail to the feathers. This preen oil keeps the feathers supple and weatherproofed and helps inhibit the growth of fungi and bacteria. Sunlight acts on the oil spread over the feathers and charges it with vitamin D, which is eaten along with the parasites and dirt when she preens.

At the same time as Merak's new feathers are growing in, I begin to notice that her delightful scaly legs and feet have a fresh new yellow to them. The small patch above her black beak, called by falconers her "scape," also has a heightened yellow to it. Before my eyes, she is coming into her maturity.

⌒

As our acquaintance with the hawk unfolds, so do the questions. Morgan, taking a break from his book, asks me whether her beak might not be getting too long. And I am bound to worry about this, for birds' bills are precious. They are tools used not just for eating, which includes the catching, killing, carrying, and cutting of food, but also are necessary for preening, nest building, excavating, egg turning, defending, attacking, displaying, scratching, hatching, and climbing. How can we tell if Merak's bill has grown too long? What can we do if it has?

I stand by the barn, watching her very awkward, stiff flight, and wonder whether it is the imbalance of her newly sprouting feathers that constricts her, or whether she has been damaged in some way. I have been unable to forget the harm she might have done herself crashing into the village house back in the spring. I am keenly aware of how vulnerable even normal hawks can be.

Author Dan O'Brien's Dolly flew into a wire, hurting her wing temporarily and her vision permanently. T. H. White wrote bitterly of the end of his experience with his hawk, Gos:

> Nothing is more certain than that Gos entangled his jesses
> in one of the myriad trees of the Ridings, and there, hang-
> ing upside down by the mildewed leathers, his bundle of
> green bones and ruined feathers may still be swinging in
> the winter wind.

One day recently Merak's droppings changed color, from a large, messy white splash with a small dark center, to a patch of bilious green. I had read that this was a sign of ill health but cannot decide whether or how to intervene. Normally, urates, a combination of the excrement from a bird's digestive tract and kidneys, are pure white, and together with some clear, watery material, make up the bulk of the feces. The fecal wastes are small, well-defined ovoid brown bodies, embedded in the white urates with which they are ejected. Often the first sign of ill health is a change in a bird's droppings, usually to green, in the colors of urates, or by diffusion of the fecal matter in urates.

In a pinch I could always turn to Kit, but, since she lives at a distance and cares for many more urgent feathered dependents, I am unwilling to disturb her unnecessarily.

As often happens, these questions are ones that will be re-
solved with time. Over time her beak stops growing and serves
her well, and she proves quite capable of righting any temporary
imbalances in her digestive system. Meanwhile, sharing my pain-
ful learning process with the hawk's, I am being taught over and
over again that usually the best and only help I can offer is to
stand by.

That very afternoon Small returns home early in a ruinous mood,
and I assume that she must have had another run-in with the
bird. No sooner do I lie down for my rest than I hear Merak
clanking on the picnic table (the sound is made by her numbered
bird band, which she treats like a bracelet, flouncing it on her
wrist). Small and I go to the window to take a look and there
is Bird, ripping an old ball (surely intended to represent Small)
crossly and conspicuously. From the safety of indoors, Small,
grand and oblivious, declines to watch, and stalks off to sleep
in my workroom, out of earshot of the destruction. Cat and
hawk remind me of two imperious feuding queens.

Our store of pictures is swelling. We are discovering how much
our bird appreciates water in summer. No doubt the water cools
her, but it also helps to damp down the parasites that inevitably
share her body. It was July when the hawk first investigated the
plastic wading pool I keep filled for our dogs to cool off in. For
nearly a month, she never returned to it, at least when we were
watching. Then, at the beginning of August, I catch Merak in
what she tells me is now *her* wading pool, spooning water up,
slaking thirst with up-turned beak. The up-tailed dipping reveals
her beautifully frilly underparts, fluffy white feathers like downy
pantaloons.

Merak also is partial to our garden hose when, as so often happens this drought summer, we are watering. "It's like a snake to her," Barry explains. At first tentatively and then ferociously, she snatches at the wriggling hose, seizing it in her arched feet. I fear she might puncture it with her talons, but watching more closely I discover that really she is trying to grasp it rather than rip at it.

The next week Barry and I have to be away for three days. While we are gone, Jeremy becomes preoccupied with other interests and pays little attention to Merak, beyond faithfully giving her her daily mice. When we return, we find that all her good humor has deserted her. She has reverted to acting devilishly and is acutely, annoyingly possessive again. She spends much time filing and preening her beak on the edge of my window box. When little black Kitty stands up indoors at the kitchen window to peer out at her, she fluffs her hackles until she becomes a giant bird hunched evilly among red geraniums. Kitty, of course, is raging. Merak's eyes really can appear either malignant or benevolent, depending on her mood. In fact, she generally has a highly theatrical aspect, posing and gesturing like no other creature I've seen.

⌒

As this first summer of the bird wears on, I begin in my mind to call it "the summer of the hawk," but not just because of our adventures with our wilful and capricious raptor: there is a relentless, hawklike cruelty to the heat and drought which withers the grass to brittle kindling. The razor heat is clean and merciless, bringing a talonlike suffering that reminds me of the unreasoning, relentless savagery of our predatory bird. Far more relentless and bitter, though, and equally inescapable, has been the experience of my special friend Leslie's leukemia, from which (I can scarcely believe the words enough to write them) she is dying. Waking one August morning to the usual livid skies and the smell of dust, scarcely laid by the scant dew, I write down a dream I have had near waking:

> I dreamed that this morning we were in court watching Merak's fate being decided. In the cold, lofty room, all was reduced to gray, black, and white. An utterly indifferent expert doctor pronounced that she couldn't go on. While I watched, he held her and scanned her contemptuously. "She has . . ." and he listed parasites. I felt the despair of hopeless, powerless misery. Then the doctor took her across the court to a room full of cages and thrust her into one and attached a label to the cage, stating that she was to be destroyed. I felt a sorrow verging on anguish.

In waking, I know that the dream is metaphorical, expressing my grief for Leslie. Yet the dream also helps me to recognize that our beloved child bird dwells ever in the realm of metaphor. She stands for so much more than she is in herself.

This morning I can't stop feasting on the sight of her, and when Jeremy brings her over to me, I get her on my fist and can hardly bear to leave her. On such a morning I am convinced that she isn't completely wild—she is too silly, so I don't regret her being our friend. Oh Merak, I love you. No, "love" isn't the right word. There are days when I heart-wrenchingly, hopelessly scan air and tree continuously for sound or sight of you. Life loses its brightness without you.

⌒

We continue to be a release area for some of Kit's birds. In August, Barry drives to the Avian Care Foundation to pick up

44

a pair of young marsh hawks (harriers) and a wounded great blue heron. Herons, being terrified of captivity, do very poorly in treatment. This one had refused to eat, so reluctantly Kit has decided to release it, even though its leg remains incompletely healed. When Barry opens our station wagon's gate, the heron is bundled in an old blanket, with its long, polished beak of ebony and yellow projecting limply on the car's floor. Clutching it warily (we have been warned that the heron's beak could easily poke out one of our eyes) we loose the protective and confining blanket from the miserable bird and slip it free by the edge of a pond. In spite of its trauma, it flies instantly, with its crippled leg dangling, and disappears completely.

The young harriers provide quite a different kind of experience. When I first peer inside their carrying box, I have difficulty believing that these immature birds really are kin to the large gray-backed and white-breasted marsh hawks who often cruise our water meadows. The pair are strikingly handsome, with vivid slate and orange coloring, but their immature autumn plumage makes them look sinister and exotic. They have owl-like rings surrounding their eyes and a small, round yellow spot on their beaks. I am surprised to see them sharing a box, but Kit has explained to Barry that they are brother and sister and have been raised together. When we push back the flaps on their box the male takes off promptly, headed for a large leafy tree north of the barn. But the female lingers in the tall field grass, breathless and panting, probably from fear, until, afraid she'll lose contact with her brother, we shoo her off in his direction. If I harbored any hope that the harriers might stay in our territory, it is short-lived. Merak, who most uncharacteristically has remained pecking around in the driveway instead of flying off about her business (I almost could be persuaded to think she knew that alien hawks were coming), now rushes, outraged, to survey the release from her barn roof. She then pursues the timid female to a large dead oak at the field edge. With the superb flight of a now fully mature and refeathered hawk, she challenges the young intruders with loud screams but, we are thankful to see, does not back up her threats. The harriers quickly vanish into the northern woods, but our own hawk, in a foul mood because of the invasion, loiters near our house all day to protect her territory.

That summer we see no more of the young harriers, and it is probably just as well, considering our resident hawk's jealousy. However, a full year later, Barry and I walk down to the distant beach late in the afternoon. It is September and we are reclaiming the lovely wooded half-moon of the beach for our own now that the tourist season has ended. We sit close together for a long time, just listening to the gentle slip and fall of the small waves. Scanning the peaceful lake, now free of noisy, racing motorboats, we spot an osprey, its wings lit by the low sun as it cruises toward the distant point of the crescent. Then, surprisingly close to our own patch of shore, Barry catches sight of a northern harrier sitting in a dead elm. But the hawk is not alone. Only a minute later a second marsh hawk flies up from a swampy nearby bay and joins the first in its tree. Any previous marsh hawks I've encountered have always been healthily wary, preserving a wide distance between themselves and humans. These two birds, however, stay serenely within yards of us for the better part of an hour. In fact they are so untroubled when we cautiously approach them for a closer look, that it is impossible not to wonder if they couldn't have been the pair we had released, now in their adult plumage. At least one of them is wearing a leg band, but even still, we will never know for sure whether either could be one of our two who claimed this beautiful shore for themselves.

⁓

By late August, Merak is a different hawk. Now sleek, plump and assured, with most of her body feathers grown in and with half of her long, reddish tail feathers fully grown as well, she spends much time posturing, evidently getting the feel of her new equipment. She is extraordinarily flexible in the twist and stir of her feathers. Confident and at ease, she shows up every day but one for three weeks and is friendly with everyone. Moreover, we begin to have more hope of her feeding herself. On different occasions, Barry sees her pecking a turtle out of its smashed shell and, at a time when no cats were out-of-doors, finds a half-eaten red squirrel on our picnic table.

This month Jeremy spends a week in Toronto at Zoo Camp, where he skips the planned activities to haunt the falconer there, learning tips on hawk management. Now Merak, still showing off and delighted that her favorite "bird" is back from camp, lets Jeremy hold her on his wrist. Polished after experience with eagles at the zoo, he grasps her legs, bossing her up on his fist, and we are impressed by how competently he handles her now. We are finding that the urge to carry her is almost instinctive. When Jeremy has had enough of her, he transfers her to my wrist. The hawk is happy and feels solid, yet hollow; I sense her balance and glowing featheriness.

But even on her best of days, she still sports a perverse sense of humor. After all our petting and carrying, she hangs around, circles, hovering over the barn, teasing our other animals. She routs the for-once innocent Small from her lurking spot in the vegetable garden's cosmos patch, swaggers up to Annie, the boss member of our Cardigan Welsh corgi trio, and finally blitzes young Rosie, the black-and-white puppy, making her yelp. Barry rages at her and in exasperation claps his hands fiercely, near her head. Offended, she later declines to accept his proffered blade of grass. But, as usual, her temper is short-lived. Soon afterwards she does consent to take a conciliatory white corn-flower from me.

At the same time that we are watching our hawk mature physically, if not mentally, we are beginning to face other kinds of changes with our own sons. Ever since I had read a compelling article by American home-schooling advocate John Holt, I have tried to persuade our sons to leave what I am convinced is a toxic school system that corrodes teachers and students alike. I keep hoping they will want to learn at home. Each autumn I have urged, "Are you sure you wouldn't like to stay home this year?" Alas, each year Morgan and Jeremy have been sure they would not. School itself is detestable, but they would be too lonely if they stayed home. They also fear that they might get in trouble with authorities.

And so the nightmares, the frustration, the lack of time to do the things they care about have continued. But this year, Jeremy has come to Barry and me and said with a sober maturity quite new to him that this, his last year before high school, he wants to spend at home. However, the wave of relief that he won't be confined in an unhealthy environment and my delight at the idea of the choices this opens up to him are mixed with some alarm. At last my theories will be put to the test. And as with Merak, there are the questions: Will Jeremy work hard enough? Will he regret the decision? Be bored? Be lonely? Will his continual presence be a burden for Barry and me, keeping us from getting on with our own work?

Talking it over with Jeremy, we decide on a model for the year. He wants to be a biologist, so he will need to go to high school the following year, where he will be able to take advantage of expensive laboratory equipment. To prepare for this, we decide that he will need a good grounding in what school boards call "core subjects," such as math and English, and we plan to divide these between us. In the evenings, Barry and I will work with him. Mornings Jeremy will do assigned work, some on core subjects, and some on additional subjects that he will choose as he becomes interested in them and pursue for as long as he wishes. He also will be able to focus on one subject, such as math, for as long as he is interested in it, and then will switch to working intensively, and at his own pace, on another. The afternoons he will have free to read as he pleases, to make things, and to go outdoors and play with his best friends, Nathan and Matthew, who fortunately also will be learning at home. Naturally the days can be infinitely flexible since only the schedules of a few people are involved. If Jeremy needs a day off, or if he wants to do something else worthwhile, such as visiting the traveling International Bazaar to look at ethnic crafts, or going on a field naturalists' outing to band birds, he can easily make up the required subject time later. The three of us are looking forward to a fluid, natural schedule, but most of all we are looking forward to an adventure.

⌒

Meanwhile, much of our attention continues to focus on Merak. I worry because I have not seen her soaring. None of us has ever seen her performing that magnificent and effortless flight, and from the looks of her uncertain, clumsy maneuvers, despite her new maturity, she has never done so. I had supposed that she has been hampered by her captivity and her summer of molting, but when September comes, I begin to wonder if imprinted hawks perform this most magnificent of flights at all.

Buteos such as Merak are built not for speed, but for soaring. They certainly sense, and may be able to see, thermals, which develop on warm days with relatively light winds. They also sense the lift to the air that occurs wherever a steady breeze moves upslope, or impinges against long lines of trees, cutbanks, or cliffs. Land birds are mainly static soarers. They use updrafts of air to buoy their bodies and rely on the air moving past their wings to provide lift, rather than using their forward motion to generate a flow over the wings as in normal flight. Buzzards, such as redtails, soar on updrafts along the faces of cliffs and hills.

Land soaring generally takes place where there are convection currents or thermals. These are updrafts caused by the air being heated at ground level. Such uneven heating causes bubbles of warm air to rise from the ground. Each bubble is like a ring that spins as it ascends so that a stream of air rises through the center. By careful maneuvers soaring birds can keep a constant position, relative to the thermal, or climb or descend. Their speed through the air is very slow, and, to prevent stalling, the primary feathers are spread so that each acts as a narrow wing. The widely spread primaries allow air to slip through and reduce the turbulence.

Soaring allows a red-tail to remain airborne with little expenditure of energy at a height of a few thousand feet where its sharp eyesight can keep a vast area under surveillance. The hawk can also travel long distances by rising as high as possible in one thermal and gliding to the next.

I discover I can guess at Merak's height when she is flying. In 1911 the German ornithologist Friedrich Karl Lucanus developed an ingenious method of estimating these heights by suspending life-sized images of certain European birds from a balloon. Knowing the height of the rising balloon, Lucanus could tell at what heights the birds were still distinguishable. A bird similar in size to a red-tail was distinguishable at one thousand feet, was a spot at twenty-six hundred feet, and disappeared at thirty-three hundred feet.

One day, after returning from an afternoon drive and doughnut-fetching excursion with the dogs, I go behind the house to gather in the washing I had hung to dry. After a week of hard, near-frost days, this is a day of dreamy hazy blue and is warm enough for shirtsleeves. I automatically glance north of the barn, as I so often do now, searching to see whether Merak is with us. There, much higher than I've seen our bird fly, I detect a gracefully circling red-tail. Could it be? Surely not. I don't dare say her name aloud, lest I distract her, even if she likely is too high to hear me. I watch the lovely, perhaps not quite perfect flight, hoping it is she, and half-fearing it might be, because that would mean that she is beginning to distance herself from us. And then, from the midst of that long time and that great sky, she sees me. I hear her sweet talk, as remote as that of high-flying migrating geese at night, and she begins to drift, in amazed circles, toward me. Clearly she is undecided, wants to come down to talk to me, but doesn't want to lose her new bliss. Apparently unsure about landing, she considers first the barn and then a telephone pole, but the wind is too abrupt. After a brief uncertainty she cruises successfully in to the broader target of the cottonwoods, from which she and I exchange stares of wonder.

In these moments of watching, I have come closer to experiencing flight than I ever would have believed possible. In my profound empathy, I actually have been riding in the heart of Merak.

But because of her newfound ability, I now begin to wonder more seriously whether she might migrate after all. Joyous as I am in her new acquired skill, my sadness at the possibility of her leaving is acute. Meanwhile, modest, pleased, the bird sits on in the cottonwoods, preening her splendid new red tail, examining and caring for her miraculous feathers with a new regard.

Because they are large, clumsy hawks, red-tails have to conserve energy while searching for food. Most of their hunting is done from a lookout perch, and even when they hunt by flying, they expend as little effort as possible. However, as Frank Beebe points out, when they finally do attack their prey, they do so swiftly and with fierce tenacity. Normally, these hawks do not chase other birds, but because of their size and nerve they often intimidate birds and other raptors, robbing them whenever possible.

Experts think that soaring provides a way to search both for territorial intruders and for food. Hunting red-tails generally do not rise higher than one hundred feet, because small prey does not remain exposed for more than a few seconds and attack must be quick. Not swift hawks, their top speed in flight is thirty-five to forty miles per hour. However, they can spot a food source from two miles or more and may well fly a mile high to scan a larger area. Red-tails hunting from four hundred feet are almost certainly on the lookout for larger prey.

The following week I spend an awesome, alarming several days watching Bird soar with migrating turkey vultures and marsh hawks. At first I am surprised to see Merak relating so readily to what previously she had seen as intruders. But my books tell me that the only other raptor usually tolerated by red-tails is the turkey vulture. The exception, they say, occurs during autumn migration, when hawks are known to associate freely in mixed flocks. Now Merak takes her place among the other hawks with a remarkable assurance: "I'm one of these." It is intensely moving to watch Merak's new, beautiful flight, and gratifying to see her choosing to be with her own kind and accepted by them. But I can't help fearing for her if she were to migrate. It is only right that she should be wild. But could she, who is so unafraid of humans, who apparently still is unable to catch sufficient food, survive without our protection? Indeed, she has become so bold that when Barry is working with a school class, she scares some of the teenagers by crashing their picnic lunch in search of hot dogs.

One afternoon, glancing out the sun porch windows at the orange-red sumacs sprawling on distant rocks, I am disturbed to see Merak very closely circled by another bird. I dash out, only to lose the two in the piercing sun. While I am standing there, with just broad afternoon shadows surrounding me, I hear, but cannot see, wild geese calling their anthem. And then the hawks pass beyond the sun and, seeing the two together, it is all too easy to catch a difference between the wild and tame. The alien one has sharper, surer strokes than Merak. There is a hardness to his gestures, while Merak is softer, more tentative and wondrous about her flight. Also, unlike the other hawk, she still doesn't keer while flying. I glance away for only a minute, but when I look again, the two have gone. Only a little while later, when I step outside to listen to another flock of geese, I find Merak returned to her barn roost. In spite of her encounter, she remains solitary in the midst of all this flocking, and I am sad for her.

In the third week of September the other raptors move farther south. The skies begin to grow empty while Bird remains loafing about. I meet her in the hanging elm at the pond when I return from town with the mail. Sometimes she seems to wait there at the end of the driveway deliberately, dog-fashion, expecting us to arrive home. When I carry wash baskets out, she flies to her vantage on the barn pinnacle to watch me. She, who had been so clumsy in early summer, now clambers up there competently. A few minutes later I see a flash of her lovely rusty coloring in the low sun and she is off to land splendidly on a twisted bleached pole of a tree. It is from perches atop posts or poles that red-tails do most of their hunting in areas where rodents are their chief prey. How I wish I could spy on her when she is roosting in her pines at night.

On weekends, Jeremy and his friend Duane practice archery and slingshot shooting around the hay bale target Barry has made them until inquisitive Merak lands on the hay and tries to join in. Zestily she rips at the bale, casting hay all around her, and when Jeremy shoos her off, she seizes an arrow from the ground and refuses to give it up. When her antics fail to divert their attention, and the boys start shooting with another arrow, she resorts to hopping up and down in front of the target, making shooting impossible. When Jeremy and Duane become thoroughly huffy about her spoiling their fun, she tries to make up with them by climbing on exasperated Jeremy's shoulder and preening his hair. Finally, totally frustrated, Jeremy and Duane leave for a walk through the orchard and, like an impossible little sister, she tries to come too—for some reason mainly on foot!

A few days later, I am wandering through dreamy fields filled with amethyst asters. I pause amid the searching autumn light, watching the fall blow away in radiant bursts from milkweed pods and the downy stars of asters gone to seed. With all this drifting, there is a haloing blurriness set against the hard clear light. There is also the new softer sound of wind in bare branches. When I stoop to watch our honeybees harvesting nectar from the flowers, I discover frequent patches of down, hawk down, left over from Merak's molt.

Then, looking up, I discover what has become a common sight, Merak soaring. Wings outspread and fingering the wind, she reminds me of the Hiroshige print of the bird flying down-sky, brooding the world. She looks down at me with a rare mild and beaming eye, surely expressive of amazement at being able to fly over the world. Once, while she was soaring, Jeremy whistled to her and she responded, sinking from the very dome of the sky back to earth, slowly transforming herself from a wheeling dot into our own familiar hawk. Today, though, I have no wish to repeat this miracle, being content simply to watch her flight. To fly through the wings of a hawk is like flying through a kite, only far better.

⁓

On the last day of September, Morgan has brought his friend Jeff home for supper, and it is so warm that we take our spaghetti outside to eat at the picnic table. Without thinking, I had given Merak a small nip of raw hamburger just before we went out, and she remembers it. I am beginning to discover that migration time seems to invoke the same sentiments in the hawk as molting. Contrary, brash, and inspired by the hamburger, once we are seated outside she warns us loudly, and then coolly cruises over to the picnic table. I gently fend her off with the large white plastic tray, but she ignores me and makes a perfect landing between Jeff's plate and his milk glass. Clearly her intention is to stalk through his dinner and on to the other plates, and it is with great difficulty that even hawk-master Jeremy manages to coax her away. That dinner has to be eaten indoors, and I make myself a mental note that I will have to refrain from miscellaneous handouts before she becomes a serious nuisance.

∽

Only a few mornings later we have our first frost of the year. When I go out with the dogs for a morning walk I meet Merak, who is a wretched sight, cold and wet, with her feathers fluffed out like a lion's mane. Just an hour later when I return up our laneway, I pause to look at the gray clouds of dissipating frost that are like shading to the robin's egg blue sky. Outlined against this sky are the already bare branches of the ash trees.

Then, across the horizon, trees flash white wings. Like a wind-driven cloud, a hawk is skimming the treetops; could this wondrous, capable bird be Merak? She is so sure, first cruising the bases of the trees, then flapping and twisting up among the ash branches. So far as I know, no other hawks are left to us here, and by now Merak is familiar with the challenges of every tree and pole in her territory and is able to land in the most improbably airy treetops.

Nevertheless, in spite of her growing prowess in flight, Merak remains inept with her landings, often slamming her feet down any old way, with a thunk far louder than one would expect from so light a bird. I have no way of knowing whether wild hawks are similarly rough, but I have been warned that hawk feet can be delicate. When she perches on our front porch's flat railing (an uncomfortable hold for her, because it is not rounded to the cup of her foot), we begin to see her clenching her right foot into her breast.

Birds of prey have powerful feet, with strong, sharp, highly curved talons and roughened pads on the undersides of their toes to help them to grasp prey readily. To me Merak's particular feet look as sound as ever, but, aware that a hawk with foot problems is finished, I coax the ever-resourceful Jeremy to consult an expert visitor at his Junior Field Naturalists meeting. The man merely laughs, saying that it is very common for hawks to rest on one foot, particularly to help keep warm, and he advises Jeremy to tell his mother not to worry.

～

Jeremy's home schooling is turning out to be a deeply satisfying experience for all of us. Although there have been occasional sharp confrontations about the lack of fulfilment of assigned work and, as we had suspected, the process does demand much of our time, while we prepare to help Jeremy we are finding that we are learning ourselves. Perhaps you never really know something yourself until you have translated it for another to understand. French, for instance, has taken on a new flavor for me as we read aloud together, or watch Sol, the enormously expressive French clown who appears on educational television each morning.

Jeremy and I read and write poems, devour legends (which have never been taught in school to either boy, and which they had no time to read independently when school squandered so much of their time and energy), grow plants while studying cytology, and go on a geological expedition. But even more valuable is the liberty Jeremy has to explore the countryside with Nathan and Matthew, the three of them finding their own most secret trails and discovering reptiles for Nathan, the herpetologist, to examine. One home-schooling book is called *And the Children Played*. What is most precious is the time Jeremy now has available to play, to explore, and to experience freely, when his energy is good, and the day is at its most pleasant. However, it is clear to me that Jeremy indeed is learning—in particular he is mastering the techniques of how to learn for himself.

Principals have actually told me that the most important aim of school is to prepare children to live in a competitive, routine, nine-to-five adult world where there is a high degree of obedience. Watching the healing and generative potential of the boys' unstructured play, I am more vehemently convinced than ever of how wrong that approach is for children and adults.

On a tender mild Sunday in late October, from far away comes the exquisite call of a loon. I am walking with some university students who are surprised that I am not more angered by things like the presence of duck hunters shattering the peace at the lake, and this helps me to see that living with Merak is helping me come to a sense of what is in my hands and what is beyond them. Last year at this time, when the leaves fell, the new openness revealed a tangle of rich green rose vines seeded with tiny scarlet berries against the brown of fallen leaves. Then, the newly emerging rose vines were charming, something to look for on each walk. This past August I found that the rayed, yellow flowers of elecampane, which in recent years had been thriving, were being strangled by the vines that I had found so beautiful. Today I show my new friends the tangle of rose vines, thriving grape vines, virginia creeper, and bittersweet newly opened by the recent frosts. Since I prize the elecampane which is being choked out, I should look on the vines as a threat. They are parasites that will weave shut the little glade. Knowing the rose vines' unfortunate reputation for invasiveness, I should persuade Barry to have his summer crew rip them out before they strangle further. Instead, I explain that I am finding that I am content to watch their progress with a detached sort of interest. Often now, I am recognizing how many things are outside of my sphere of control. As we continue our walk, there is the sweet lisp of bluebirds in the pale air.

One day, while I am going over some papers, I am shocked to see Merak fly straight into the living-room window. Horrified to think what I might find, I surprise myself by the celerity with which I get myself outside. Fortunately, in spite of the force of the impact, the hawk is unhurt. But I am puzzled by this inexplicable behavior. No cats were present to tempt her to charge. Had she seen her reflection and supposed it was a rival hawk? Was this some sort of dispersal routine such as grouse go through, where those seemingly crazed birds go to any lengths to escape from their previous territory?

Three days later, the weather is cold, windy and inhospitable. There was sleet yesterday and today snow flurries. I hear another bang on the living-room window, and I am incredulous. Surely this could not be Merak again? I instantly dash outside once again, without even taking time to grab a coat, and find a small grouse lying stunned on the lawn below the window. Before I can think what to do, nearby Merak gives one pleased squeak and, in a flash, sails in with a breathtaking display of flying and grips the luckless bird competently in her talons. She can't concentrate on her prey with me observing, however, and I want the stunned grouse to be killed quickly, so I reluctantly retreat to the house. In spite of my leaving, Merak withdraws with her prize to the privacy of the backyard thicket of plum bushes. Later that morning, when I look out toward the bushes, the wind lifts away the grouse's only remains, a stream of small feathers, like air bubbles from a fish.

At October's end, when I had thought all other hawks had left, our bird has one more territorial dispute to weather, a suggestion of what she might face the following spring if she can survive our winter. It happens on a dark day, when patchy snow lies on the ground, while plumper-than-usual bluebirds flutter among the juniper berries. I am listening to the cold rain ripened by the calls of many migrating birds, when there is a brief, miserable cry from Merak. She glides in from the orchard, low and uncertain, ending up on the porch. I had been noticing that in migration time, the little birds who challenged her last summer ignore her, and now, when she appears, only the robins find it necessary to tattle. Standing at the window, I am surprised to see another hawk fan into a landing in an aspen in the slight swamp behind the barn. There are a few more fussy cries from our bird on the porch. Apparently, now that she seems to have made a decision to stay here with us, she once more finds other hawks threatening and turns to the house and its humans for protection.

Now a second intruder joins the first in the swamp, and, as I watch, the pair (for plainly they are a pair) of red-tails soar briefly, wings touching for a moment, and then land in a dead elm at the back of the first field. If it is true, as I have read, that soaring is as much a territorial display as a means of hunting, this pair may be challenging our hawk's claim to this area.

Poor Merak flies to our telephone pole, where she sits defiantly, but she is within safe range of the house and wheeps very gently to herself. The other birds now retreat, cruising skeleton trees, past high, wind-driven clouds. Evidently they will respect her and skirt her miniature territory around the house.

Just then comes the first howl of that northwest wind we had been promised. Bird, I think, had better get herself off to her pines. She has never come to us on days of high wind, and I wonder whether she will be able to reach her shelter if the wind blows too severely. A half hour later, though, she is still hunched on the pole in rain, her dappled cream breast standing out against the gray sky, determinedly defending her home.

Her home. Indeed, she has become fully at home around us— sometimes disturbingly so. She has become a Peeping Tom. In the summer she peered in our bedroom windows, coaxing us to join her in her distressingly early rising. Now she takes over my window box, sheltered by the back porch, as a vantage point from which she can watch the family and its doings through the kitchen window. Having seen me fetch her thawed mice from the fridge and then deliver them out to her, I suspect that she knows exactly what a fridge is for. She gets quite excited when she spots one of us swinging its door open. She also appears to know very well what is happening when I set out and fill three dishes to the dogs' chorus of ardent approval, and she looks understandably resentful of their good fortune. As the weather grows colder, she is becoming more insistent and bratty, flying at us each morning and sometimes heedlessly landing on Jeremy's back and scrambling up, rather than dropping neatly onto his shoulder or wrist. I still find it hard to know if she is getting enough to eat, but she looks well.

Morgan reports that Bird often sits in the gaunt dead elm we call "the hanging tree," down the lane by his pond, waiting for him to walk in from school. He tells me he bobs up and down to greet her in bird fashion, which she receives as her due. When he does so, she looks happy, he says, and makes feathery sounds to him.

◦

When the week's season of deer hunting arrives, I am deeply worried that Merak will stray beyond the park limits and be shot. Falconry began before firearms were effective, and I find it interesting that only after mechanical weapons became common were raptors seen as competitors rather than assistants. During the twenties and early thirties, all raptors were classified as vermin, and sometimes even had bounties placed on them. Autumn hawk shoots became traditional. Although such mass destruction no longer occurs, and although chicken-killing is usually the last-ditch effort of a young or old red-tail, farmers still mistrust hawks, and guns are readiest in autumn.

Merak is distressed, certainly by the powerful warlike gunfire, but probably also, with her superb sight, by the invasion of the surrounding area by howling men and dogs. The first morning, I give her a large rat, hoping to console her and encourage her to stay safely close to home. She drops down onto the lawn and mantles her splendid mature plumage to work the rat over, reminding me of a Roman emblem. "Be careful," I whisper in my heart. "Of all weeks in the year, for now be careful." And it seems that she is, for at the week's end she still is with us.

◦

After hunting season a remarkable peace falls over the area. There is a cease-fire after the necessary but hectic losses of autumn, and the newly bared landscape rests before the assault of winter.

I go out with the dogs into a November mist. Some parts of

the landscape appear muted; some, like the tracery of seed-laden ironwood sprigs, appear sharp against the dull background. Generally, sound is muffled, yet schoolchildren at the playground across the lake sound oddly near. Almost by accident, in the wet hollow at the road's curve, I notice luminous bare trunks of long-dead trees, as if one further curl of spirit emanates from the dumb silver trunks.

At the bottom of the steep hill the great stand of oaks, with their russet leaves, gives us a second fall. The odd tree or vine still is lime-colored, but the oaks' dense covering of rust, and ochre and carmine, contrasts with the reedy grace of the bare-limbed maples, whose leaves have long been gone. A heavy sky is pressing down on bright green moss. This mist is nearer to drizzle. A brief flight of birds appears veiled. And there are robins—flapping and squawking.

In these few weeks of tranquillity we enjoy Merak more than ever before. After a restless October and then the distress of deer hunting, she seems happy enough just to be near us and hangs around as she never has before. I suspect that her instincts have been tugging at her and that now, for a while, she is out of their grasp and at peace. With pleasure, I watch her soaring airily over Morgan's pond at the bottom of the laneway. Although her leveling strokes are more assured now than at autumn's beginning, after watching wild predators this fall I have to acknowledge that all her motions are tentative and babyish. Meanwhile, as a writer, I am searching to describe the benignity of her flying: "Watching the superb beauty of her flight," I write, "I feel I know what the sensation after death will be. It is as if all of earth's burden is removed. It is beatitude."

And it is these swift shifts between the magnificent and the absurd that make the hawk such a vivid presence for me. The next day, on a balmy autumn afternoon, I glance out to see our giant, hunchbacked bird wading slyly in a puddle. But it doesn't stop there. She dips her beak—to slake her thirst, I suppose, and comes up with frog legs dangling from her bill. In catlike surprise, she drops her prey, pounces, considers, recognizes that it will have to be the frog or nothing (she's had her daily allotment of mice), and mumbles the creature down. Then, the distasteful chore completed, she paddles and sips some more puddle with glee, shakes herself like a feather duster, and strides on her heels over to the compost bin to dry off.

We have also recently enjoyed the proverbial "bird on a wire." The wire stretched between the telephone pole and our house is a theater of activity. In summer a bluebird, a diminutive humming-bird, and a robin may all sit peaceably along its length. In winter, the line is colorful with crimson house finches and goldfinches in their winter plumage.

Merak, who was hopelessly gawky when she came to us, now entertains us with a fine display of tightrope walking as she teaches herself how to balance on the line. She begins by clutch-ing the wire close to the pole, and she bobs rather desperately, trying to true her bulk with the narrow center of gravity, but she never disgraces herself by falling off and in a few weeks pro-gresses to swaying sedately at the line's sagging midpoint, as much at ease as the chickadees who rest there between trips to the feeder. To our relief, Merak, perhaps aware that with her bulk she is unlikely to be able to prey on them, appears at home with the chickadees. She seems content to crane her head to study them with a placid eye.

When humans visit her territory, she unerringly appears. Whether she sees herself as defending her territory, guarding us, or simply keeping the new people company, we can't decide. But so showy are her arrivals that she seems to be announcing herself: "You're going to really enjoy this. Here I am!"

❦

Disgusting! Really gross, as the boys might, and do, say when in December we give Merak her first muskrat carcass. While winter hunting, with longer nights, extends the time frame for night-seeing hunters such as owls, it is just one more restriction for a hawk living on the northernmost edge of the species' wintering territory. With shorter days, and cold that devours a hawk's energy, Merak's need for additional food becomes urgent.

Overwintering is dangerous and difficult for birds. Small species like chickadees are particularly at risk of freezing. They have proportionately larger surface areas through which they lose heat and so must eat continuously during the short daylight hours to stoke their metabolic fires. A wintering chickadee, living at minus four degrees Fahrenheit, must spend something like twenty times as much time feeding per day as it would in the warmth of spring. Although Merak has a larger mass than chickadees with which to retain body heat, she needs food-given energy to support her extra weight.

As fierce cold sets in, we recognize that we must do something to help. It isn't practical to ask Kit for a steady supply of mice for our dependent hawk; she has her own problems finding sources for her own birds. We have found that the fresh roadside kills of rabbits or squirrels, used by many to supplement captive hawks' diets, are hard to come by on our little-traveled roads of winter. After much mental rummaging, we hit upon the idea of substituting the remains from a trapper's winter kills. Gerry Mulville, a friendly neighborhood trapper, is glad to offer us the skinned bodies of the muskrats he has caught for their fur. It really is a commendable idea, we tell ourselves. Nothing will go to waste. It will be a muskrat recycling project. And so it would, if only the hawk could be persuaded to accept the foreign objects as food. And the bodies *are* foreign. Indeed they are the most revolting objects I have been unfortunate enough to see. The lumps of dark, bloody flesh are bereft of every animal quality except teeth and tail.

I gag my way out the kitchen door and pitch the first blood-dripping carcass onto the now empty flower box, where we have been feeding Merak for the winter, and wait. Expecting mice, she rushes in, squawking and flapping, but draws herself up short on the flower box's edge: "This is not my food. What would I possibly want with this?" However, disgusting or not, she quickly decides it must be hers, and claims it with an outstretched claw that warns me to stay back. For the better part of a cold hour she broods over the repulsive carcass while I hover anxiously at the window. At last she decides that muskrat is exactly what hawks like as a supplement and sets in to devour it. In fact, the first two days she gorges so heartily that her crop looks ready to burst. After her feeds she actually has to waddle to the picnic table. Thrifty as ever, even when the flesh is eaten she picks diligently at the bones, which will yield her needed minerals. And we are thankful. At least now her winter's food supply will be assured, although we still have no way of knowing how she will survive the bitter cold yet to come.

After her great feed she is in high good humor, where the past week she had been shrill and fractious. I didn't believe she was catching much on her own now the cold weather had come and take this easing of mood as an indication that she had been truly in need of food.

Although I now have graduated to doing most of her feeding, Merak prefers males. But even among males, Jeremy remains special for her. And his instinctive movements with her are so right and understanding that it almost seems as if he knew her in another life. The weekend after her muskrat orgy he plays with her—a silly game of chase across the lawn and a one-sided hide and seek. "She cheats by flying high to see where I am," he protests, rushing panting back to the house.

⌒

Then, in mid-December there come a few days of exceptional cold. One night, while there still is no snow to protect the ground, the temperature drops to minus twenty-two degrees Fahrenheit. The next morning, with frosted eyelashes, Merak shows up for a rat. (I hadn't known that she *had* eyelashes.) She is fussy—partly unhappy, I suppose, because of it being a rat day instead of a muskrat one (I am alternating her food) and partly because of the harsh weather.

A few days later, when Merak doesn't appear, I am swamped by a deep, sickening sadness. The air is impoverished, the trees barren. There is a relentless sparseness. Yesterday I went out on the porch, which was cracking with the sudden hard frost, to pet her and was relieved to see her feathers cupped and well-oiled and even a few crystals of ice on them to show how well insulated she was. She didn't seem to me deeply troubled by the cold then. I turned away from the sharp wind to return indoors and heard the reassuring taffeta rustle of her feathers. Ten minutes later I glanced out, hating to see her ice-lined eyes, even though they apparently didn't bother her. As I watched, she took off for the barn roof, but because it was dusted with snow, she landed midpoint and, to reach the peak, she had to resort to the silly, ungainly scrabble that she had performed when she first came to us. Later that afternoon, I saw her fly surely off to the north.

Since then I've been searching for a reason for her disappearance. Yesterday at dusk Jeremy and Barry heard two unfamiliar owls talking around Morgan's pond. Indeed, Barry saw one of them, which he said was fairly large. Is Merak disturbed, as she had been earlier by intruding red-tails? Has she hidden? Has she now decided to move south (which seems unlikely), or has she met with an accident? Her poor performance on the barn roof yesterday does little to reassure me that she can take care of herself. Or, most likely of reasons, has the harsh cold been too much for her? "Falconers do lose their hawks, all too often, and always with such a downward somersault of the heart that it almost suffocates them." I recall these words of British author and would-be falconer T. H. White, and my heart sinks.

I hadn't meant to go out this morning; it is so cold that even the corgis aren't insisting on a walk. But now I think I must go alone and call Merak. It is foolish but, with visions of her tangled in a tree or freezing to death, I must.

Grief-stricken, I walk the points of her compass—north to the oak behind the barn, south to her roosting pines, east to the dead elm behind the orchard, and west to the hanging willow by Morgan's pond. Everywhere there is beauty and affirmation, from the upsweep of silver milkweed pods to the rime of frost on the field grass, and, in spite of the forbidding cold, there is life. There are chickadees everywhere and blue jays call over my head, but all are pale shadows of Bird. On my way to her pines, I find a mound of frost flowers—frozen breath from a warm burrow. After an hour, for the last station on my search, I stand beneath the hanging tree, thinking how she so often had sailed in to meet me there.

Without her presence to remind me of the often foolish qualities of a human-imprinted hawk, I am drawn to reflecting on her holiness. While my face searches the bitter sky, I think of hawk-centered creation myths. I think of the Melanesian great bird god Tabuerkik, who soared above primordial chaos and beat it into life with the wind from his wings, and also of the North American raven who hovered over the earliest sea, fanning it into life with the wind from his wings. On this morning, to me, Merak is this raven. I am surprised by the force of my discovery of how much poorer the air seems without Bird. Without my knowing it, she, like the raven, has become a life-evoking force for me. For ancient Egyptians, the bird Horus was the symbol of the soul. In knowing this half-wild hawk I have glimpses of the soul of the world.

The gleam of a distant plane and the line of its arc are scars across the otherwise empty sky, and I turn in failure to go home. Then, from I know not where, I hear an indignant cry and see the beloved, difficult bird fly past the house. In my heavy snow-boots I clump back up the driveway and am in time to see her mount the chimney top. When I reach the house she is roosting like a phoenix amid the chimney vapors. I show her a muskrat, but there is no response except a few indignant cries: "Yeah. What? You called me? So what have you got for me?"

Barry, who has just returned home for his morning tea, says, "Let me take care of this," and he whistles for her. Grudgingly, she flies to the telephone pole, but still refuses to come to the porch for food. When we go back into our warm house to put the kettle on, however, she is attacking her muskrat methodically. She's fine, excellent, and I have learned that Merak can weather the cold. Now we think it may have been she who killed the rabbit that Savannah, the gray, white, and tan corgi, had brought home yesterday. The old buzzard is splendid.

On a January afternoon, untroubled by the continuing intense cold, Jeremy, Nathan, and Matthew come trooping back from the nearest, and recently iced-over, beaver pond with an unbelievable story. "We walked over to have a look at the lodge, now the ice is safe, Mom. It's still that black ice, you know, where you can look down inside the pond and see all the weeds and everything while you are walking. But Mom, you'll never guess what! You know how Dad said there aren't any beaver in there this winter; well, he's right. Nathan found a way into the lodge. It had caved in on one side, and so we all crawled inside. We were inside the lodge, Mom. It was much bigger than we would have thought." Jeremy was almost too excited to talk. "It felt like we actually were beaver. We were inside looking out."

⌒

Early in February, Gerry, our trapper friend, brings Merak a present of two beavers, hoping she will accept them as a substitute for muskrat, which at present are scarce. I try to look at the gift simply as thirty-five pounds of rich, oily, hawk-preserving meat, but, as Barry lugs one out to her, I can't help seeing the carcass for what it is—fat, draped like a flounder, and only resembling the doubled-over, rounded muskrat corpse in the grimace of its yellow teeth. The paddle tail, so eloquent in water, makes up a surprisingly small part of the body, while the arms and legs are puny, like flailing baby fists. The head, when at last I bring myself to look, is full of holes. There are eye sockets and nose cavities, rounded and ripely empty like those of an ancient Inuit mask.

To me, a well-fed and sheltered human, the nakedness of skinned creatures is raw and wounding to see, but Bird receives this strange gift, not wheekingly but regally, extending a talon to claim it after much weighing of its merits. Now that muskrat season is closing, we are anxious to switch her to beaver, but her pecking turns out to be half-hearted and ineffectual. Each day for a week Barry lugs the hulking carcass out to her feeding flower box, where, each day, it gradually freezes. Each evening he wraps it in a garbage bag and places it in our basement to thaw overnight.

However, at the end of the week I stroke Merak's breastbone, my only way of guessing at how well-nourished she is, and am shocked by her thinness and weakness. We have to face the disappointing fact that Merak, catholic eater of grouse, chipmunks, rabbits, snakes, crickets, worms, grasshoppers, frogs, and carrion, firmly and irrevocably dislikes and declines to eat beaver.

Frank Beebe has noted that red-tails are highly adaptable and can survive on remarkably small amounts of food. One young wintering bird, he writes, survived over five consecutive days with no food, and indeed, on thirteen of twenty-one days it ate nothing. Its ability to have a total intake of less than three and one-half ounces per day was an important survival factor for the bird.

Nevertheless, so anxious am I made by the faintness of her talk and her unfleshy bones that, for the only time in my life, I actually wish for a microwave oven, so I could hasten the warming of frozen mice to replace the spurned beaver. Instead, I have to settle for putting them, carefully wrapped, in the warming oven, a process I would never previously have condoned.

～

Returning from a late-afternoon walk, just a few days later, through a blur of whirling snowflakes, Barry and I see Merak sailing in toward the hanging tree. She sinks with grace onto the elm's topmost stump. A minute later it is sunny, with a sky of delicate drifting clouds and when we reach the house, snow is rushing in avalanches off the roof. I've been thinking that in another month a mate might come for Merak. But actually, the changes begin far sooner than I had expected.

Long before we can sense spring's coming, on the day after Valentine's Day, as if a switch had flipped for her, she begins nest building. Barry is astonished to find Merak, babyish as ever, fidgeting a few sticks about on our front porch. It dawns on him that apparently this public and unsheltered place is her idea of a suitable nesting platform.

A week later, Merak is continuing, after her own fashion, to work hard on stick plucking and gathering. In her usual haphazard way, she alternates between days of purpose and days of mooning in the cottonwoods. Her energy expense has been so great that over the winter we have discovered that there is a cutoff point of coldness after which it is very difficult to keep her sufficiently fed. Now, however, in her broodiness she is less interested in food, and though there still are days of acute cold, she appears to need less food and is less fluffed out to keep warm.

Red-tails generally start nest building in late February or early March. Several stimuli, such as length of day, rainfall, temperature, and availability of food, initiate this urge. Usually nests are sited in mature forest, in a location that gives an incubating female a commanding view of the surrounding territory. Both the male and female participate in constructing a large, bulky nest, with a sturdy base of heavy sticks, but the final shaping is done by the female. She uses her wings, beak, feet, and breast to squish down a lining that may consist of the inner bark of red cedar, grapevine, corn shucks, or long grasses, materials that will help insulate her eggs. During the several weeks after she completes the nest and before she lays her eggs, the female lingers alone around her nest, and often perches on its rim. A typical nest might be thirty inches across and four to five inches deep.

With an eye to safeguarding the precious heap of sticks, the hawk begins to suggest to the dogs that they are unwelcome. In defense of her eyrie, while hotly chasing the innocent and twittering Savannah, she even once flies between the bars of both sides of the porch, a considerable feat for such a heavy, clumsy starter. Reluctantly, we decide that the dogs will have to come in the back door for the duration of nest building. How we will welcome any visitors unwise enough to approach the front door and how fiercely they will be driven off remain to be seen.

Luckily, she doesn't consider her human family to be a threat, so I am able to spend a happy half hour lying on the porch stairs, crooning to her and taking her picture. How I wish I could understand her thinking. Does she include us as part of her colony, since her nest is attached to our house? Sometimes I even think that this creation is an offering for us. In return she graciously accepts our gifts, and we take to bringing her a few choice sticks each time we return from a walk.

The nest takes on a definite pattern. What began with heavy branches is refined with the addition of small twigs, mostly yanked from the nearest trees, our cottonwoods and plum bushes. To these she eventually adds evergreen branches, which she resourcefully tugs from our old spruce Christmas tree. Later I learn that such evergreens, which contain natural pesticides such as hydrocyanic acid, may actually act as an insecticide.

⸻

Our hawk's relationship with the other nearby creatures remains complex. One day we see her perched on one of my empty hollow-log planter boxes, tail feathers fetchingly uptilted, as she rummages in it. But why? Soon it occurs to us that a chickadee lightly hit the window moments ago. We had paid little attention; judging from the impact, we assumed that the bird would be stunned but unharmed. Might Merak have nabbed it? Sure enough, when she rights herself, she flies off with a limp, fluffy gray-and-black bundle dangling from her talon. Dismayed, I wonder if this will change her attitude toward chickadees, whether she now will see them as prey.

But it doesn't. Barry has figured that when in a tree she ignores squirrels (sometimes as many as two black and four red ones will scramble boldly about on the branches near her) because she can't move well enough to catch them in the entanglement of branches. This may be true, and may apply equally to the small birds at our feeder, but I can't forget the agility with which she dove under our porch last summer when chasing cats.

In general, as naturalist and author John Terres has pointed out, large adult hawks do not try to catch small birds, who are too agile. In fact, he theorizes that small birds actually are protected by their proximity to a large hawk, because smaller bird-eating accipiters, such as sharp-shinned hawks, do not venture near a large hawk. This fluctuating relationship with prey was also noticed by nature writer Edwin Teale:

> In their relations with their prey, predators often appear
> to obey certain rules, as the knights of the Middle Ages
> observed the codes of chivalry. In the far north, goshawks
> have been seen remaining unmoving for long periods until
> a ptarmigan they were watching took wing. As soon as the
> bird was airborne, they plunged and picked it from the air.
> In this instance, the goshawk waits for the dove to fly. But
> the dove does not fly. Thus the smaller, defenseless bird
> escapes. There apparently are limits to the predations of

every predator. Skating on the thin ice of these limits, its
prey often insures its own survival.

～

Certainly, over winter, Merak's flying has gotten rusty. It appears
that she understands instinctively that keeping warm and hunting
expend too much energy, so she restricted her motion and left her
winter feeding to us, as do the birds at the feeder, who desert us
the very day the weather improves. Now, however, if there is to
be renewed hope of her becoming self-reliant, she will need to regain her flying skills.

On the last day of February, a day of warmest sun and muf-
fling hoar frost, I meditate further on our hawk's chances at independence. After her shorter winter hours, when she frequently
didn't even appear until ten o'clock or later and flew off to her
roost by four o'clock, she now, sensing spring, or in a hurry to
get to her nest, comes early and stays late. It remains impossible
to gauge her abilities. Barry discovers drops of blood on the snow
beneath her perch. Has she been hunting? Yet on this February
day she displays all her infantile, human-imprinted qualities. As
I am writing, she tries to clutch her way onto the narrow window
ledge of my upper-story workroom. Composed in spite of her
impossible perch, she stares at me insistently. I mull over her
ever-increasing presence anxiously. Frequently she is even a danger to herself. Earlier this morning I caught her skating gingerly
and unwisely on the hoary branches of our trees. Then there are
sickening beak-over-feet and wings-every-which-way tumbles
when she slips on the barn's tin roof or misses a tree landing.
Every time I hear a rush of snow whoosh off our roof I worry
for fear our not-quite-real bird has become just a heap of permanently disarrayed feathers, smothered in a pile of snow. I know

she can fly and land superbly if she puts her mind to it, but so often she is heedless and clumsy. Instead of cutting her speed ahead of time, she flops down heavily with a thunk that must surely shock her fragile yellow feet. So much of her behavior remains babyish—she displays the querulous talk and the flopping and flouncing of a chick. And yet sometimes her eyes soften to a gentle wonder at the fineness of being a bird, and I once again am committed to helping her seek out the wildness that is in her.

There are implications for us, too, in our continuing relationship with the half-wild hawk. Only a few days later, on the afternoon of a dark, bleak March day, I experience a flash of rapture as the first crows return from the south and fly cawing to our cottonwoods. Anxiety soon follows, though, as I hear a piercing wail from Merak. The crows have invaded her territory and are harassing her with unexpected boldness. As with living with children, it is hard to share her life yet not interfere.

She, on the other hand, has no qualms about interfering in our lives. If, with her nest, she becomes more possessive of us and the house, and hence more aggressive with the dogs, I am not sure how we will manage. And what about the cats? It is nearly time for them to start going out again, but will they be able to get out at all, with the cat-hating hawk patrolling?

⌒

And this nest-building is progressing apace. After two tries at a nest of under a dozen sticks, each blown away by an unkind wind, Merak has gotten more steadily to business and has built a large mound of sticks. What sort of sticks does she choose? Many she plucks from the cottonwood. (We've seen her cling, squirrel-in-spring fashion, to the tips of unlikely small branches, ripping them off.) There are spruce branches from the discarded Christmas tree, which has protected our lavender plants over the winter, a pussy willow twig that must have come from a distant pond, as none of the willows at nearby Morgan's pond are blooming yet, and shreddings of bark, also from the cottonwoods. Between Merak and the red squirrels, these poor trees are looking haggard.

Over many days she has laboriously squished down this untidy litter of branches into the jute doormat, which she uses as a base. The whole affair is pushed as close as possible to our front door and she has even tried to suggest, stick in beak, that it might be better if she were to transfer the nest indoors. One day last week she strolled past Morgan into the living room before he could shoo her out, possibly hoping to disarm him with her nonchalance. Even when she remains properly outside, there is much clashing of beak against door, whether to hint that she wishes to come in or because she is working close to the door I can't tell. For the past week, she has been arriving at the nest at six-thirty, when she begins singing to herself and, unfortunately, to us as well. She rarely leaves the immediate surroundings of the house anymore.

We still have worries about feeding her. In theory, she is just being lazy and we should learn to let her fend for herself. However, when her breast feels hollow when I stroke it, and when she becomes feeble, I worry. With difficulty we coax a few last muskrats from Gerry and one last bag of mice from Kit. Next year, we tell ourselves, if she still is around we will have to make arrangements with trappers for a reliable source of muskrats before winter. In the meantime, we recognize that once fair weather comes we will have to stop feeding her. I find myself wondering if she will still come around. Although I hope she will become independent, I know that I would like her to remain trusting with us so that we can help her if she needs it.

⌒

But all the while, in spite of the questions and concerns, the vignettes that make it all worthwhile continue. Morgan comes to breakfast, laughing at having seen Bird sitting in the cottonwoods, surrounded by a host of little birds—chickadees, nuthatches, finches, and sparrows. She was watching them softly, he said, looking as if she wished she could talk with them instead of being a solitary hawk. At supper the same day, a chickadee stuns itself by hitting the kitchen window. We bring it in and, as is our habit with dazed birds, tuck it in a cake box to revive it in warmth and darkness. Fortunately we have acted promptly, because Merak briskly appears from her lurking place on the roof. "It was mine. It was mine. It was supposed to be mine," she protests. The chickadee revives quickly, as they often do, and soon makes vigorous feathery sounds. We are able to slip it safely out another door, on the other side of the house from the still-indignant hawk, but the business of befriending other birds remains a difficult one.

⌒

April 3 is a highly significant day. The previous day Merak was making increasingly distressed cries. I had vowed that when the snow was off the ground and hunting easier I would not feed her anymore. But, when I stroked her to test her well-being, so upset did she seem, and so gaunt, that I was tempted into presenting her with a large rat. This she seized in her talon, but then she did what she never has done before: ungraciously flew off without eating it.

Today, after heavy rain and fog, our friend and Barry's colleague, Leanne, comes home for supper with Barry after the two have been teaching maple syrup collection and production at another property. As we usually do with visitors, we show her Merak, who once again is lurking on the back porch. While we all stand looking at her, we see another red-tail soaring in the orchard, no doubt the first of the returning hawks. However, uncharacteristically, Merak doesn't seem to notice. The sky is clearing and the evening is full of promise, but Bird appears very fidgety, and even twice screams harshly at us, although her serene eyes show she isn't serious. After supper we are setting out on a walk to show Leanne the waterfall in full flood, when we make a surprising discovery that explains Merak's recent misery. She has laid a large, whitish-blue egg in her nest and is nursing it!

Afraid of disturbing the nesting mother, we hurry off on our walk. But we need not have been afraid. All Merak's customary flightiness has been dispelled by her new responsibility. Even when we go to bed, she remains faithful to her egg, bravely hunched down in front of our door, looking small. Does she realize how vulnerable she is, sitting out in the open, within easy reach of any passing predator? After nightfall, she could be particularly at risk because hawks are supposed to be incapable of the night vision needed to make an escape.

Without telling Barry why, and in spite of a cold draft, I insist on keeping the bedroom window open that night, and I sleep lightly, listening for sounds of a struggle. We know from the corgis' nocturnal barking and from the opened compost pail we find each morning that the raccoons have awakened from their winter sleep and have returned to their customary evening raids. My fear is that, in fighting them for her precious egg, she might be wounded or killed.

And this morning, in spite of my wakefulness, there is evidence of a possible tragedy. Hurrying out to the nest first thing, we find the egg smashed and no Merak to be seen. For the next half hour, until she appears and feeds greedily on the last muskrat of the year, I feel apprehensive. There will, of course, be no explanation. We will never know how the encounter played itself out, or by what unusual power the threatened bird managed, in the darkness of a moonless night, to make her way back to the safety of her pines. By nightfall, Merak is calling again—another egg? a mate?

Five days later a second egg appears and Bird is proving to be a good mother, baring her warm breast to it, staying with it faithfully. (Eggs are held against the brood patch of the incubating parent, an area on the breast that loses its feathers and develops a rich supply of blood vessels.) With no mate to spell her, how will she manage to brood her egg and raise her babies? (Fertile, chick-producing eggs are only possible if mating has taken place, but, unlikely as it seems, we cannot be sure that Merak has not mated.) We are not to find out how our hawk would cope, however, because when I look out at ten that night, once again the nest has been raided and, once again, Bird has somehow managed to fly off into the dark.

Whether she wishes it or not, Merak's nesting has apparently been discharged for the year, and she is at liberty again to explore the possibilities of being a free bird. Now, after the long winter and her responsibilities as a parent, she has begun soaring again. Just the very tips of her wings are upturned, like hands reaching for the zenith. The flight feathers are her fingers, spanned out as far as possible. Gentle. Amazing.

After her long spell tied to her nest, Merak can turn her attention to potential invaders of her territory. Two nights before she laid her second egg, Jeremy went for a twilight prowl, back through the orchard to the lane leading to my friend Elizabeth's farm. When he returned, he told how he had been met and chased by a red-tail which he thought had come from sitting on a nest in a pine. Because the weather had been poor for the first half of April and I had been preoccupied with Merak and her nest, I had not been paying much attention to the avian arrivals away from the house. When at last I am able to have my window open, I am drawn outside by a distant keering. Merak is working over her muskrat in the flower box, so I know the caller is a second red-tail, and I walk out across the field to watch. The hawk circles up the sky in steps, higher than I'd imagined possible, until it reaches a pinnacle where it becomes a speck to me. This alien hawk sweeps along with draped feathers, covering her realm as Merak covered her nest.

But unfortunately the coming of this hawk means that the fields surrounding our house no longer belong to Merak. Once again, our great bird, who at first had rejoiced in her freedom from parenthood, becomes fussy and restless. She hangs around the house nearly all the time and squalls miserably, although apparently not for food or attention. During the egg-laying fit, she had seemed to cry for food, but then had been edgy and puzzled when we gave her some. At that time I had begun to wonder whether she might have confused her unfamiliar mating/nesting urges with hunger. But now, with the egg season past, I must look for another explanation.

Merak appears to welcome turkey vultures. Last fall she learned to soar with them, and now she occasionally joins in the circling of the trio that visit us, though always careful to maintain a small distance from them. But plainly she sees the approach of other hawks as invasive. By mid-April, the first hawk in the skies is joined by a mate. Evidently the new pair disdains Bird's claims to her territory. Their territorial soaring comes as close as the far side of the barn, and poor Merak flaps impotently, able to guard only the small area between barn and house. It isn't until two weeks later, at the month's end, that the rival pair begins to stake their infringing territory less aggressively. We, and undoubtedly Merak, still see them hunting every day, but the rivalry diminishes.

Near the end of April it still is fiercely cold with a hard north wind, so we give her an immense white rat for her breakfast. First she pins and claims it with her foot, and then takes it away, talking pleasantly to herself. That evening, Barry meets her in the driveway, and Merak chats and plays with the rat's remains, highly pleased with herself and life. On the last day of a month which had seen so many changes for her, I notice Merak flying by the open window, clucking softly to herself as she goes.

She has become easier at last. She comes around far less, but is chattily friendly when she does. Visiting Jeremy and his friend Nicole on Saturday afternoon, she actually mounts Nicole's proffered arm. It is the first time she has allowed a stranger to take her. Sunday she helps Barry weed the asparagus patch, her help consisting of tossing strips of bark about. At supper time I catch her on the porch, pushing the dogs' tennis ball about with her beak and yanking mischievously at my new doormat. Then she steps down and patrols the porch's latticework, teasing Small Cat, who is lurking underneath the porch. I suppose that this interest in teasing the cats, rather than hunting them, must be taken as an indication of well-being.

⌒

And now it's a quarter to eight at night; the treetops are golden with the last sun. Knowing that Morgan soon will be leaving home, I have begun making a "freedom quilt," a leaving-home quilt for him, and it is pleasant on these brighter nights to stitch at it. I stop sewing to look out the open window for the geese I've been hearing. Instead, on an outermost branch, I catch sight of Merak languidly fanning a wing, then sleepily stretching a leg. Five minutes later, when another flock of geese passes by and I look again, she's left to roost in her pine tree. Good night.

⌒

Early in May when I unwrap our bees from their winter protective covering, I am discouraged to find mold and a mouse nest. Both are suggestions that the colony had not been strong enough to care for itself adequately over the winter. It takes much longer to check and clean up the frames than I had expected, so I am glad when, drawn by curiosity, Bird flies in. First she flounces among twiggy bushes, then, with bold disregard for the dancing bees, lands on the open brood chamber. Here she picks admiringly at tidbits of wax. After she tires of helping, she catches and eats two worms. Indeed she keeps me company the whole time I am replenishing frames.

⌒

Even in May, the weather continues to be unpredictable, as does our hawk. On a Saturday when she and the weather are mild, I go out to sit with her on the immense circle of tree trunk, once a chopping block but now used as a step up to the porch. Taking up her scaly, yellow foot in my hand, I admire her talons, thinking they look like the water-dark, streaked soapstone of Inuit carvings. By Monday it is unusually cold again, with ice reforming on puddles, and Merak is in a sour mood, screaming and stamping, buzzing past when I take the dogs for a walk, bombing Rose and willfully flicking my cheek with her wing.

After the walk, while I stand on the porch drying the dogs, she joins us, flying in with alarming force before she puts her aerial brakes on hard at the last minute. It seems to me that a hawk, with a hawk's fragile feet, should leave no room for mistakes with landings. But now that spring has come, often, when mounting the metal barn roof or landing on a telephone pole, she is negligently imprecise, slamming into her target and scrambling and flopping the last distance needed to achieve her roost.

I still have flashes of despair for Merak when the intruding pair of red-tails circle skillfully over her territory, causing our hawk to figuratively wring her wings. At such times she remains unable to settle until they vanish into the northward sky.

Soon she has another reason for discomfort. Early in May, when I walk out to listen to the song of a nearby white-throated sparrow, I am surprised to find a large feather in the violet garden. Merak is beginning her molting much earlier than she had the previous year. At the same time, I am disturbed to find her beak is flaking, and I wonder if she could be lacking some essential nutrient.

Spring continues, an uneven but ever-tantalizing procession of rough and smooth. Although it is as dark as an early April night, there is joy. A cold, clear rain is falling, accompanied by cold, clear birdsongs, but everything is tingling with expectation—on the verge. Merak is mounted on the clothesline pole, shunning the shelter of porch or pine trees. Tonight she is happy, shaking herself with contentment.

But even while I delight in the rainy night with her, my anxiety about her health continues. She seems to have lost much of the oily waterproofing from her small, soft head and breast feathers. I consult Kit's husband, Robin, over the phone about her scaly beak and lack of oil, but, faced with more serious cases, he doesn't know what to do. I wonder if I may have to experiment with calcium and cod-liver-oil supplements, and speculate on how to get them into her. Talking with Robin, I do get one point clear, however. On hearing about her egg-laying in the nest by the front door, he finally agrees with me that our unfortunate hawk must be human imprinted.

On the first hot Friday night, we try to have a picnic under the trees, but Merak is up to her old tricks again. As usual, when she approaches she has her "You're going to like this! Here I am!" look. We can't agree though, as she sails in to land feet first in the spaghetti, and she is mortified by our loud annoyance and subsequent evacuation to finish our supper in the house. We wonder if we will ever be able to eat outside again. After supper, when I go out to fill the compost pail, feeling somewhat contrite about our earlier harsh words (Barry had even shaken a broom at her), I find her on the lawn, punching ants with her fist and looking simultaneously both wise and foolish.

Unfortunately, the cats' springs during Merak's reign have not been happy. Small, capable as usual, quickly learns Bird's full measure. She has worked out the hawk's flight angles, and knows exactly how to slink about openly without fear of attack. Mainly, though, she is content with a lair under the back porch. Also, except when she rightly gauges Bird's mood to be at its worst, she coolly ventures out around the house. Modest, but matter-of-fact, she continues to ask to go out each morning, and spends most of the day in the confinement of her latticed sanctuary.

Alas, little black Kitty, timid as ever, only rarely makes it out the door, although from within the safety of the house he sings desperately of his longing for the outdoors. Usually, if he is to get out at all, we have to catch him and chuck him out. Once through the door, though, he actually travels farther than Small, heading down to the safety of bushy, sheltering junipers around the beehives. Unfortunately, he then is trapped there and has to wait until Bird's withdrawal at dusk. Then he wails for me to walk down, tug him out, and carry his limp, shuddering body back to the house, hidden in my shirt.

In a tempting stretch of warm weather when Kitty seeks the junipers three days in a row, Bird becomes wise to him and in the evening threatens to refuse to leave the cottonwoods for her distant pine tree sleeping roost. She lurks about, delaying her customary departure until the last light is leaving the sky, making us wonder if she will spend the night trying to outwait me and Kitty. In the last remnants of twilight, she apparently feels compelled to fly off while she still can see to do so. More than ever, I wonder how she managed to leave her nest in the darkness after the raccoon raids on her eggs.

One night, I am talking to my mother on the phone and looking out the open window. I am idly watching the swallows skimming about the barn when I hear a muffled, feline-sounding scream and spot Merak grappling with a writhing bundle on the other side of the driveway. Horrified, I motion to Jeremy to run out to discover her prey and possibly avert the kill. He rushes back, wide-mouthed to announce that, completely unaided, Merak has caught a large snowshoe hare and has deftly wrung its neck with her talons—a classic hawk kill, driving the talons of the contracting foot into the victim's body. Certainly I have to admit that the scream was brief. Unlike the struggles and games ensuing from feline "kills," Merak's dispatching of the hare was amazingly quick and effective.

Red-tails generally hunt unaware prey, the small mammals and insects that tend not to look upwards. However, they are skillful enough to vary their techniques to suit their prey. For instance, they have been observed approaching a rabbit by surprise, gliding in one direction, and then turning back to take advantage of the cover provided by a small hill.

Although we pity the hare that had to die on a lovely spring night, we rejoice in Merak's prowess. But, alas for the hawk, the story has an unsatisfactory ending. Normally, a hawk would take its kill to a "plucking post," a safe spot where she could rip off feathers or fur and then tear into the flesh. But the hare is heavy, and Merak is inexperienced. Hunched over the body, where it remains on the ground, she gorges her crop, and then flaps heavily into the twilight, leaving what is left for the morning. However, afraid that the raccoons will carry off the remains overnight, Barry lifts the body on a shovel and puts it in the barn. He means to return it to the hawk the next morning, but, in the rush of getting ready to meet his class, he forgets. Later that morning Chris,

Barry's student assistant, goes to the barn while doing a garbage run of the park and discovers the remnants of the hare. He reasonably assumes we want it gotten rid of and takes it away. Supposing that Barry had restored the hare to Merak as he had planned to do, I am unable to understand why she dives at Chris and me all day with screams of outrage.

⁓

On the traditional seed-planting day for our region, May 24, on an afternoon that is warm, still, and hazed, I plant seeds for early vegetables—carrots, beets, lettuce, and beans. Merak supervises, looking down on me from the back of the barn roof. For the first time since last spring, the lesser birds, the swallows, robins, and phoebes, now at the heat of their territorial protectiveness, scold her furiously. Bird, however, vain as ever, takes their protests as compliments. Busy patting the seeds into the furrows of cool earth, I don't pay much attention when Merak drops down behind the barn. However, when I hear her crunching noisily, I become curious and discover that she is halfway through gorging on a large milk snake. She never does finish it, but, when sated, wipes her beak lustily on an old fence rail and flaps back up on the barn roof to follow my progress. That night, Barry returns to the garden to wrestle with the choking grass in my iris bed. He is assisted by Bird, who, in the process, polishes off twenty worms!

The night when Kit phoned to ask us if she could release Merak at Foley Mountain, we said to ourselves that if the hawk proved to be human imprinted she might be able to help with Barry's conservation-education program. It would have been a considerable asset for Barry to be able to call down a hawk from the sky to his wrist, so children could approach it. As with our former wild pet, Fanny, now that Merak has become a reality we have to recognize that our hopes are unrealistic. The hawk is too infantile and unpredictable in her behavior to be trusted with classes. We decide that she will have to remain our private source of joy and information. However, having so interesting a resident hanging around the house, it is inevitable that visitors will be drawn to her, whatever our plans. The following Sunday, in spite of wild, gusting winds, we find ourselves calling on the hawk to put on her first public performance, a show for our teacher friend Fran, her sister, and her sister's little boy. We all huddle on the porch and Barry calls Merak, who is perched on a nearby pole, by proffering a mouse. To us, the hawk seems a little fretful with the high winds, but on the whole she takes the attention well. Our visitors are captivated by the beautiful big red-tail who so deftly cuts across the fierce winds on her way to the porch. At that moment I begin to wonder whether it might be possible after all to share her with a wider audience, when we have developed a more comfortable understanding with her.

After that blustery day come clear, warm days of late spring, of lilacs, more than I ever remember flowering here, and apple blossoms come and gone within four days, petals flying in the wind. Merak, too, is mild, tender, genial. At last she doesn't need to loiter by the house all day fussing. Sometimes she only appears at three o'clock and then only for an hour. There are times, though, when she still is full of defiance and distress about the intrusion of the other red-tails. One evening Jeremy walks back through the now long and blowing grass and finds an alien hawk defending her pine tree nest. He even thinks he sees a chick reaching up out of the nest.

As with all her moods, however, Merak's distress is short-lived.

Quickly she forgets her troubles and becomes fetchingly easy, gawing and playing silly games. She shows off by pitching manure clods in the garden or by shredding plastic planter boxes.

⌒

When other predators search our fields, we can appreciate the something that is lacking from our wild-living hawk. At June's beginning, Merak and I watch a fox pouncing among the deep grass, a beautiful picture. I hadn't believed the fields could be so tawny, nor the fox so fieldlike. However, what interests me is that he moves with a rapier-sharp attentiveness that is missing from our hawk's general attitude. Merak, on her pole, abuses him, but alas, his initial respect for her quickly fades as he recognizes her essential and deep-seated childishness.

⌒

With the coming of June, Merak's landscape has changed. Her trees are different now. It becomes harder for us to find her among the abundant leaves, but her piercing eyes continue to search us out effortlessly, whether we are outdoors or in. If we happen to be indoors and out of sight, she squawks to us appealingly in the all-too-early spring dawns or during my afternoon nap. To our relief, in the evenings she gives up lingering until dark, so it is easier for the cats to get home for their sunset supper. Small still usually lurks under the verandah, but Kitty, the more fearful of the pair but also the more desperate to be out, has learned to streak to freedom by means of a series of safe spots. First he races across the dangerously unprotected yard to our car, then to the more distant truck, and then to the sanctuary of the snowy-petalled cherry trees that surround the beehives. Small, in her verandah sanctuary, is becoming bolder. One day Jeremy sees her step up on the porch and swear at the nearby hawk quite openly. Bird still can be deadly; we all know that. But, because Small stands up to her, Merak and the little Siamese cat appear to have an understanding.

⌒

Quite unexpectedly, at this point a new character joins us. Long ago I had made myself a firm rule never to read a humane society's newspaper column advertising animals in urgent need of adoption. In spite of myself, however, all too often I "just have a look." When, to my surprise, I see a bluepoint Siamese listed, I shock myself by taking prompt action. Several years before, we had had Mia, a dainty, affectionate bluepoint kitten who had been the only one of our animals ever to disappear. We never knew whether innocent Mia had willingly gone in a stranger's car, or had been seized by a predator, but we grieved for her gentle, friendly presence. I had always been drawn to Siamese for their intelligence, charm, and deep affection, but I had difficulty with the idea of buying a purebred cat when so many mixed-breed ones needed homes. If I adopted a humane society cat, I could assuage my conscience and have the cat of my dreams as well. Within half an hour of reading the ad, Morgan and I are at the shelter.

Taio is not the cat we had expected. Although he is indeed a bluepoint, he is a homely one. He is startlingly large for a Siamese, and his eyes are sunken in his forehead. Nevertheless, when I see him hunched in his cage I know we will have to take him. Even when the manager, who obviously loves this cat, warns us that he had been previously adopted but returned because of his unpleasant and excessive singing, I am uncharacteristically determined. "Other than the voice," the manager tells us, "you'll never find a better cat. He gets along perfectly with every cat here, and he loves people. I often have him out to sit on my desk."

On the journey home, we are introduced to the voice. Perversely, I happen to like Siamese singing, but even I would have to admit that Taio's voice, a bellowing howl, is astonishing in its power and endurance. The manager is quite right about his friendliness, though. While earlier introductions have taken as long as a month to take satisfactory effect, our four cats find it impossible to defend their territory for long against so amiable an intruder. Assuming the best, Murray (Jeremy immediately christens the new cat "furry Murray" on account of his woolly behavior) simply proceeds to insinuate himself into the well-established pile of sleeping cats on the bed. What can our cats do against another cat who is cheerfully oblivious to their foulest threats, and who, if the worst came to the worst, with his impressive size, is fully capable of protecting himself? By Murray's second afternoon with us, he saunters into the bedroom where I am having an afternoon sleep and shocks the other cats by matter-of-factly butting a tunnel under the comforter and settling down to stay. So far so good, but Murray still has to meet Merak, and when it comes, the introduction proves to be nothing short of spectacular.

Shortly after the big cat joins us, he is sitting in Morgan's window on a muggy night, singing a Siamese-ish song to the misty sun. The hawk, possibly inspired by the prospect of a new victim, and certainly impelled by more than even her usual share of mischief, virtually says, "For me?" and sails into the thin screen, claws first. Understandably shocked, poor Murray makes a frantic dive which sends crashing first Morgan's large fan and then his desklight as well, smashing the bulb but leaving its base jammed in the socket. Out in the hallway, the terrified large gray cat bowls straight through Jeremy and whisks under our bed, where he remains for the rest of the evening. From that night on, Murray decides that he would prefer to be an indoor cat.

~

What a difference three weeks make. When I planted my seeds in May, the swallows, robins, and phoebes had just begun to object to Merak's generally innocent presence. By mid-June, the birds' territorial instincts have become feverish. Swallows scream at Merak and ride on her back when she sails off her barn roof. Robins yell and snitch wherever she goes, and worst of all are the orioles, flashing and darting and shrieking all day long. At first I feel sorry for the hawk coping with the onslaught, yet soon I see that, in spite of being under siege, she continues to look serene, as if she is accepting praise that is her due. She glances at the birds that ride her back as if they are nothing more than tiresome mosquitoes.

~

One morning the hawk has one of her occasional absences. At eleven, just after I have seized the chance and pushed the reluctant yet wistful Kitty outdoors, Small saunters into my writing room and jumps onto the window ledge. Only minutes later the cat startles me by making a rush at the screen. I hear the softest, smuggest gaw, look out and up, and see scruffy red tail feathers projecting defiantly over the edge of the gable. (The red of these feathers is an unmistakable rust, like Indian pigment.) Apparently happy and at ease, Merak is enjoying tormenting the cat as a change from being tormented herself by the nesting birds.

~

Meanwhile, Bird's weeding, which at first we looked on as charming, has become a huge nuisance. When Kit learns that the hawk has been eating worms, she warns us that we must put a stop to the practice, because we don't want to expose her to a possible parasite. While she believes that red-tail systems may reject "syngamus", or "gape worms," the nearly inch-long blood-sucking nematodes which reside inside the trachea of birds, she thinks that we should not take the chance.

Unfortunately, the more we insist that Merak leave off, the angrier she gets at our completely unreasonable behavior. She hops and stamps and scolds; Barry whacks her lightly with weeds; she sneaks and pounces. Bent on having her own way, she even whooshes from trees to snatch erring worms from the lawn, always making sure we are watching her defiance.

⌒

Because the days of June are hot, we decide to try once again to have supper outdoors on the picnic table. "Oh good," says Bird, who has been hanging around the house all day wheek-wheeking, partly because she hasn't had a mouse and partly because her molting makes her out of sorts. She lands professionally on the table and heads straight for my plate. Patiently, Jeremy coaxes her onto his wrist and carries her off to sit in the trees. Not unexpectedly, she flies right back. "Look, you," says Jeremy, determined to be obeyed. He seizes her like a fowl, hands around her wings, legs dangling, and marches her to her feeder (our window box) at the back of the house. Outraged, she returns to the tree, and flounces her way up it, but she turns her back on us to show that she is offended. There never was such a creature for displaying high dudgeon.

⌒

By late June it is insufferably hot and humid. What with the heat, her now escalated molting (the first red fingers of miniature replacement feathers are showing in her tail), and the continued occasional encroachment of the more sophisticated pair of redtails, Merak is wretched. In her misery, she becomes very poor at taking care of herself, flinging herself against the barn roof, only to be unable to drag herself up its scalding side. There is much woeful squawking. Indeed, the day-long racket is hard to take. I would have expected that on these wretchedly hot days she would prefer to keep still in the shade of our dooryard trees. Instead, she stands in the scalding sun, panting on our roof's shiny metal chimney cap and wheep-wheeping no matter how kind we are to her.

One sweltering day, I realize that my appreciation of Merak and her ways is giving me the gift of a heightened awareness of the behavior of other birds. I have seen Merak with her beak open in response to the heat, and now, when in the heat of the day I see a crow, its beak open soundlessly, flying across mirror-still Wolfe Lake, I conjecture that it also is panting.

"Any one of a thousand seemingly insignificant incidents can upset a hawk," remarks Ronald Austing, author of *The World of the Red-Tailed Hawk*. As we move into July, Merak is continually upset, and hence impossible to live with. For the most part of each hot, humid day, she hangs about in the hottest places, the dooryard hydroelectric pole or the shiny metal barn roof, making her usual miserable wheeks and a new despondent chucking. That first summer I had worried needlessly about her penchant for heat because I had read in the early falconry manuals that "in truth, heat / Quickly weakens them" and that one should "take care that [the falcon] does not have too much sun! / Indeed, I tell you, this will defile it." By now I have learned that her penchant for scorching summer roosts does her no harm.

Because of her discomfort, however, her cat war becomes relentless. Now she routinely bashes and rips screens. We patch repeatedly until the screens are more lattice than mesh, and still holes appear, holes that inevitably are followed by mosquitoes. At night we hear the whine of hundreds of mosquitoes assailing our now faulty screens.

Merak does very little soaring now, though we can't tell whether she remains grounded by her molting, the heat, or both. When screen ripping pales, for recreation she flops into the pond willows to torment the redwings that are nesting there, only to be driven off by indignant parents who ride her back until she withdraws to her barn roof.

❧

By the middle of July, Bird has become positively dangerous. Our hopes of introducing her to classes in the coming fall plummet. Previously, Merak has come to land on our wrists so gently that we have never needed to wear gloves; yet now, when Jeremy shows her to visitors, she digs her claws right through the heavy gauntlet he is forced to wear. She is also flying unpredictably. When I call her to meet another group of visitors, she roars up to me, flapping wildly, and startles me by landing, albeit gently, on my shoulder rather than my proffered wrist. When our friend David Hahn brings some of his summer company to see her, she flaps around wildly, horrifying everyone by landing on various heads, although not roughly, fortunately. Merak's persistent wheeking is driving us crazy: we have resorted to closing the kitchen curtains and hiding from her. I have tried love, water, extra food, and remonstrance, but nothing mollifies her.

It is a further difficult two weeks before her new feathers grow in, and then she becomes calmer, only visiting a few hours a day.

However, the punishing heat and humidity continue to be hard on the bird. When she does visit she spends most of her time draping her feathers and panting, open-beaked.

Taking pity on her, one night Jeremy carries her over to her wading pool on his fist. She balks at first, but he drops her in with more resolution than I would have had, and she has a fine time, sipping, splashing, and preening. The next night she hounds Barry while he is watering my flowers until he falls to temptation and sprays her instead of the flowers. After a mighty squawking, she finds she is quite pleased with the coolness. After that, whenever the hose comes out, she not only plays her pouncing, snake-hunting game with it, but she also begs to be sprayed. Soon we also discover that she is using the pool on her own. Jeremy, up early for his volunteer work at an archaeological dig, lets the dogs out prior to his departure and meets Merak, who appears dripping wet, having bathed early and privately.

———

How much a part of our lives the hawk has become. One morning in August we wake at six-thirty to drive Jeremy to his dig and there are wisps of mist over the grass. In the dim world (morning and evening light is so much less now than it was in early summer) we hear Merak gawing primitively and softly to herself in the trees—a nursery sort of sound, but also a "before the dawn of time" sound. Later, at eight-thirty, the mist has burned off the fields, but lingers in the sky. The soil's warmth is at its annual peak now. It warms my bare feet in the afternoon, and rises shimmering to make a background for the August bowers of magenta loosestrife, cream boneset, vivid orange-yellow black-eyed Susans, and dusty pink joe-pye weed. July's swamp milkweeds now have finely curving pods; September's asters are buds, already well on their way to being stars. Overhead I hear Bird's stumbling progress across the roof. Later, when I go for a walk she follows, but only to the hanging tree, her firm, territorial southern limit.

꙳

Last night, my beloved neighbor and kennel owner Elizabeth phoned to say that Maida, her Irish wolfhound, had disappeared with two of her hound babies. Over the summer, watching the puppies playing at Elizabeth's and watching radiant Maida bounding across the fields to greet me, I had lost my heart to these dogs as I never have to any other. I have always been fascinated by bridges between domestic and wild, and, in knowing the wolfhounds, as in living with Merak, I feel I have come close to experiencing instinctive wild behavior.

Maida is wild and graceful and gay and cunning and fierce in ways that have been bred out of many dogs. Although with the three Cardigan Welsh corgis we already have more dogs than we had intended, I am bewitched by the primitive nature and great heart of the wolfhounds.

It has been proving far more difficult to sell the nine rapidly growing puppies than Elizabeth had hoped. Only the past weekend, in a forlorn attempt to find homes for them, she and I had taken two of the choicest—brave, winsome Black Maria and big, soft Jerome, the largest of the males—to a wolfhound specialty show. The nine-week-old babies had shown a gentle dignity in spite of their evident fear, with Maria sheltering the male in their kennel on the truck ride down. In the beginning we had enjoyed the show, which had seemed like a gathering of soulmates. We had watched in delight the great shaggy hounds, grouped in clans in their pens, and the gaunt, ghostly heroes, coursing the distance of the field and stalking against a backdrop of forest as they were exercised before their classes. However, although there were many who were touched by Elizabeth's lovely, fragile puppies, no one was prepared to buy one.

As the morning grew long, I made up a story to distract us: "Suppose that wolfhounds are Mimis," I began. "Maybe you know already that the Australian aborigines say that Mimis are friendly spirits that live in caves. These giraffe-like creatures are said to be so thin that the slightest wind will break their long necks and long spindly legs. And indeed, because of this, only when it is calm do they come out to hunt and paint. If anyone comes or a breeze springs up, they blow on the rocks, which then part to let them enter and close behind them again. The best time to meet them is when they come out in the stillness of evening and leave messages like leaves or paintings. These Mimis were the aborigines' first teachers, who showed them how to paint and hunt. And Bush People say we still can learn from them. When you hear the eerie, soundless cry of a Mimi, and see it, so stick-like and fragile as it dances across a rock face, then you begin to understand what it is like to inhabit a truly wild state.

"Just look at Maria and Jerome, so frail and long-legged and breakable, so gentle and far-seeing. They might well be Mimis."

In the afternoon, gathering clouds promised rain, and the crowds diminished. By midafternoon we admitted that there would be no buyers, and we were glad to return the two puppies to their mother.

But now I wonder whether Maida had been distressed by the brief disappearance of her puppies and had decided to hide them from us? Elizabeth suspects that she might have taken them away from Joker, her west highland terrier, who had been tormenting the relatively defenseless puppies. But the most likely explanation, it seems to me, is that, with all her wild instincts preserved to an unusual degree, Maida had taken her children with her for the pleasure of their company on a walkabout during which she would teach them to fend for themselves. Celtic wolfhounds glory in autumn's return to brisk weather. For all their great size, soft, vulnerable wolfhound children stay babies longer than those of most dogs. Long into the night I lay awake brooding over the disappearance.

And now it is first light of the next morning, and I am drawn out to search the fields between the conservation area and Elizabeth's house. It is the godliest of days. On such a morning, in the fields and the woods, at the ripest turning of summer, it is a waiting-for-autumn time, a summer-lingering-into-fall time, a dream time. There has been a heavy dew. The steeplebushes tug, whipping a shower of dew over me. And there are more cobwebs than I've ever seen, the first of autumn. I pause to look at the swollen yellow body of a garden spider poised on the dew-limned threads of her snare, and then am brought back to the troubling reality of what I am about.

But the birds. Somehow, over the long, parched summer I have forgotten there could be so many singing. As I walk through the orchard, the slight, sweet bluebird song of the pairs who nested nearby this spring is magnified by many voices, until the orchard rings with it. Indeed the heavy air is noisy with birds to the point where I wonder if I will even be able to hear the dogs if they should happen to be near. Jays are busy everywhere; catbirds mock from all the borders of the field; flickers call; woodpeckers drum on dead elms; the bushes quiver with sparrows. And there is our own particular Bird, now nearly in full dark new feather. Surely she is handsomer and darker this year than she was the one before. Last night, when we heard that Maida and the babies were gone, Jeremy said, "If only we could ask Merak. She sees everything and surely she would know." Already, twice today, early light as it is, she has beaten back over me, trying to discover what I am searching for. Never before have I felt more keenly my differentness from the hawk. How effectively she covers the terrain from her vantage point of sky; how poorly I can search the same region from earth.

When you are looking for a creature, you have to form yourself to it. Fixed in my mind, everywhere in the wraiths of early morning mist, I keep seeing Maida—a medieval huntsman's hound of arching loins, deep chest, curled, feathery wheaten coat, proud head, hawk-keen eyes. The giant dog is vanishing in and out of the mists, courting me to play, pouncing, rollicking, roistering, thundering over the rocks. A gust of hard love sweeps through me. Elizabeth, now seriously worried that she will not find homes for the nine hound children, has promised me a puppy. If Maida's grip on me is so tight already, how will I bear the possible pain of loving and losing a wolfhound of my own?

But this morning, Maida and two of the puppies are lost to us. So aching with her disappearance am I that I actually try divining. I stretch my hands, palms tilted, drawing up all my imaginings and picturings of Maida and feeling for a way to go. Inexplicably, my hands keep drawing west, toward Elizabeth's red-roofed house. Finally I set off on the trail in that direction. There is so little I can do. I can only try to be guided by imagining her presence.

My corduroys flapping cold and wet about me, I push ahead through rough scrub, keeping the hot sun on my right brow. "Maida. Oh, Maida." My throat makes a searching sort of yelp, a beseeching bark to her, begging her to be all right and to take her puppies home. Over and over, every thirty paces or so, I lay a boundary with my voice, making guidelines, soundlines, to call her to me, to send her home, begging her to make the superbly dawning day right.

My feet, hidden from me by the steeplebushes through which I thrust, feel their way onto a deer trail, and I move more easily until I reach a dead end, a miry-looking slough choked with rushes. The cold-rising mist clashes with the scalding sun. Last night Elizabeth had wondered to me if the babies could have been trapped in such a place.

To avoid such thoughts I force myself ahead, quickening my pace, wading through the whipping dead grasses and plunging through wiry steeplebush. I will go to one more place, back across the fields through the spruce plantation and up the ski trail to the rise where in winter you can see far across the back of the park. I haven't been there all summer because I hate the thought of seeing the drought-wasted ponds. Now, tired and anxious, I can no longer dwell in the day's joy. The new pond across from Bachelor Beaver's Pond, never a good one, over the summer has dwindled to puddles and gasping mud. Even Bachelor Beaver's Pond, in other years a great sheet of water with willow-sheltered avenues and bays, has grassed over until it is a quarter of its usual size. Usually, on a morning during these last weeks before duck hunting, I could have flushed up thirty or forty ducks. Today a solitary mallard flaps up to protest my presence. I am calling continually now.

I vainly try to take pleasure in the returning lichens at my feet, restored by approaching autumn's heavy dews. When I reach the rise, I scan the broad, scrub-filled fields, wholly ungraced by dogs, and know my search is hopeless. I have done all I can and, desolated by the emptiness, I begin to trudge home.

I am pushing past a low spot, sloshing through low-lying golden pond sunflowers when I hear, coming from behind the distant Lost Pond, a trumpeting growl—just one. It is a sound in the same family as a chair abruptly scraped back from a table, but fuller. Thinking of the missing puppies, I try to avoid the thought of a bear. Could this growl have come from a large machine? The grader starting out to level the distant North Shore Road, perhaps? But there have been no other sounds of machinery this morning. Could it have been the bellow of a steer from across the lake?

But this noise is in quite another pitch. And indeed this is roughly where I have encountered a bear two other times in past years. The sense of dread which invaded me at the slough intensifies. I have been confronted by a law of wildness I cannot cross. "Maida!" I roar from the pit of my stomach, hoping to drive off the bear.

All the dismal walk home, the bluebirds still sing, and the hot sun is defeating the mists. Back in our yard, it is impossible not to return to comfort. Bird, looking wise but unhelpful, cranes forward and fluffs through her breast feathers with her beak, in all the private ecstasy of a red-tail on a fine morning that has a tinge of migration in the air.

"Elizabeth phoned while you were out," Barry announces when I wearily walk back into the kitchen. "About twenty minutes ago, I guess. She said to tell you that Maida and the two babies had just gotten back—hungry, of course, but fine."

⌒

Autumn arrives, with the same tugs to Merak's loyalty that she had faced the previous year. Although I now know that larger birds are believed to have greater cold tolerance and superior ability to fast through periods of harsh weather, remembering the hawk's first difficult winter with us I still will worry about her. Will she leave with the migrants or chance another hard winter with us?

Hawks migrate using specific routes, along mountains and ridges where thermals and updrafts are plentiful. By gliding from thermal to thermal they can cover long distances, often at a fairly high speed and relatively effortlessly. During the course of their journey, they may travel between one thousand and two thousand miles.

The Birder's Handbook identifies five primary sources of directional information for migratory birds: "(1) topographic features, including wind direction which can be influenced by major land forms, (2) stars, (3) sun, (4) the earth's magnetic field, and (5) odors." Studies have shown that young birds learn to recognize and navigate by the polestar. For travel on overcast nights, if the setting sun has not completely been hidden by cloud, birds set their course by that. If they have neither stars nor sun for information, birds will orient by wind direction, although using the wind frequently leads them to fly in the wrong direction. Pigeons have been shown to be able to detect the earth's weak electromagnetic field and can use it for orientation.

In time the other raptors pass on, leaving the fields to Bird, and she soars and occasionally hunts, with ever growing assurance. But birds migrate partly because of the scarcity of food, so we know that once cold and snow cut down on available prey, we will have to continue to supplement her feeding.

Merak may be staying with us, but this autumn Jeremy must leave us to begin high school. His ambition to follow a science career means he will need the availability of more equipment than we would be able to provide. However, from the beginning of his home-schooling year, his learning had seemed a natural extension of his living with us. Whether we were reading *Beowulf* together, examining the plastron of a turtle shell he had found, or translating French, his fresh examination of knowledge enhanced Barry's and mine, his generous and open personality brightened our days. Although we had agreed from the start that he would only be able to manage a year at home, his absences now are more wrenching for Barry and me than we could have imagined. It will be a long while before we will become used to the quieter, more sober life largely spent without him and his interests.

Always the losses, always the gains. Amazingly, there soon comes my first day with my own wolfhound. Her registered name will be Mistrale, but for now she is just Missy. Because the puppies still were not selling (more than half remained unspoken for), Elizabeth asked me if I would like one.

When I go over to Elizabeth's to pick Missy up, Elizabeth is tired and out of sorts from having to deal with an unhelpful customer. She confesses she feels the puppies are a jinx, since they began a continuing run of bad luck for her. She says that as long as they had good homes, she will be thankful to be nearly rid of them, regardless of what money she gets. "Just take whichever one you want," she says and turns back to her chores.

Faced with choosing a wonderful gift, I walk slowly and disbelievingly back to the pen under the spreading apple tree where the hound family rests and cavorts on fine afternoons. After looking carefully at level backs and well-set shoulders and haunches, as my breeder friends had taught me to, I gather up one of the largest daughters of Maida and Solomon Grundy, choosing her for the beauty of her head.

Barry and I set her on the kitchen floor in the amber late-afternoon light and look in disbelief at this Mimi that graces our home. And indeed, this is a feeling I've had ever since. I am astonished at her beauty, frailty, and dignity. Before long, our other animals become aware of the newcomer. Kitty, who comes hustling to hurdle over the gate I am using to keep the young hound in the kitchen, bashes into the puppy before he knows it and, lover of dogs though he is, is shocked to see a giant dog, a dog quite beyond his imagining of a dog, in his own kitchen. When Small, warned by Kitty, approaches the kitchen to investigate, she announces, "This is ridiculous and I'm not having any part of it."

As for the other dogs, so gentle is this new child that I really think Annie and Savannah fail to notice her at first. She is so young and helpless, they apparently decide that she is not worth bothering about. But not Rose. Until now still considered the baby herself, Rose puts on the performance of her life. She draws herself up in horror and passes as far away as possible from this dreadful apparition, cringing away from what might as well be a shadow. The act drops exactly as soon as she thinks we are not looking.

One thing is sure: the corgis know she is not another corgi. When they growl reprovingly at her, commanding her to submit by lying fawning on her side, she is willing, but insufficiently in control of her legs to cooperate the way a proper Cardigan puppy would. In her bemused way, Missy would like the dogs for friends, but is rather shocked by their aggression, noise, and bounce. The wolfhound's first night is peaceful. Missy sleeps in her kennel with the cage door open and Jeremy catches Annie, the motherly old boss corgi, administering a comforting tongue wash.

But the hound's introduction to Merak is another story, and a worrisome one. On Sunday a friend brings her corgi puppy over to visit our corgis and the four romp on the lawn. Bird notices

Maddy's (the visiting puppy's) presence. (It would appear Bird can count. She knows perfectly well if mouse number two is not served after number one.) But she smoothly lets it pass. However, a day later, she takes instant umbrage over the delicate "baby" that confronts her on the lawn. Savagely jealous of our new pet, she buzzes Missy once, talons down, and we yell. Then she attacks a second time, and poor Missy yelps and lopes desperately away from the safety of the house and down to Morgan's favorite rocks. I rush to carry her back, but between the swooping attacks and the excited sharp barks from the corgis, the trusting puppy is shaken. I try again at dusk, hoping and believing that Bird has retired for the night, or at least tired of bombing something so non-threatening. However, out of the shadows, on silent wings, as if part of the house was falling on us, swoops Bird. This is it. Missy gives up on the outdoors, especially as a bathroom.

When I take Mis outside the next morning, Bird once again attacks her hard and loudly, but this time not dangerously. So swiftly and sneakily can she attack that I am off guard. The next time, I reluctantly enlist Barry, who brandishes the broom, fending her off four times. After that she scrapes back and forth on the metal barn roof in a filthy temper. Whether she has learned to leave the puppy alone remains to be seen.

If Merak and Rose are villains in this introduction of a new and very young dog, there is also the kindness of Murray, Small, and Annie. Murray, the former humane society relic, has a pure-gold character that shines these days. If Annie, in her training, even growls lightly at Mis, the large, mushroom-colored cat is there, weaving and mediating. He seems to have taken on welcoming and heartening Mis, bringing her into our circle. When we let Mis out of the kitchen to explore the hall, Murray butts her and allows himself to be washed all over with Missy's wet

and already large tongue, then strolls along beside her protec-
tively. He has always been elderly Small's loving bodyguard and
now he curls up with the stranger at night as naturally as if she
had always been with him.

Last evening Small, who long ago brought up baby Jeremy,
joined Murray, sitting in the kitchen armchair to keep Missy
company in her confinement: "If there's a baby, there's a job for
me." Annie, too, is patient and motherly. Her growls are very
delicate, as if she senses this new daughter's vulnerability. Actually, I think there is an element of respect for Missy's size present
in all our pets, although I do find it surprising that sheer size
would worry them, accompanied as it is by so few defenses.

Two days after she comes to us, I put a collar on Missy, and
we take her for a first walk along the road with the corgis running beside her. At first, thinking leash training would be too
much for her so early, we let her walk free, but when we see
the speed with which this baby can tunnel through the roadside
grasses, I run back to the house for one. Still thinking in terms of
when Rosie was a puppy, and adding to this her gazelle-like legs,
I expected that she would quickly tire. Instead, she lopes gamely,
exquisitely, to the end of our lane and across the road, where the
six of us sit on the rocks and rest and play. She walks back well
on the leash, and plays with us on the lawn, though not yet with
the more daunting Cardigans. She is tentative, tossing her head in
that invitation-to-the-waltz that Maida also performs. While this
happy scene is taking place, Merak watches from the house and
preens herself. Perhaps the two fresh mice from Barry's traps that
morning have helped to mollify her.

⌒

Toward the end of September, the highlight of a week of hazy,
heavy days has been an afternoon ramble with the Cardigans and

Missy. We make our way back through the fields to the pine-clad campground. After a number of abortive attempts, Missy and Rosie have been able to coordinate their play and have a lovely tussle with lots of splaying of front feet in the field, while Barry, Jeremy, and I watch in delight. Missy has found it hard to settle to her food in the presence of the other dogs, so she is thin. More worrisome, though, is Merak's behavior. Her furious territoriality is terrorizing Mis whenever we walk close to the house. Barry has been challenging her with the broom and she mostly respects this, though it's awkward to hold a big clumsy puppy who looks like Pluto while brandishing a broom. Last night we ate outside and Bird even buzzed and rolled Rosie. Outraged by the hawk's new reign of terror, Barry chucked the broom up at her tree, though considerably below where she sat. She screamed her anger at him. This morning she came for her mouse and then left immediately. Are her feelings hurt? Has she learned to accept the puppy's presence, or can she learn? What can we do if she doesn't?

At the end of the month the autumn's first frost comes. There is a sharp wind and a sky alive with brilliant stars when I take Mis out with others to romp in the dark. By day Merak appears resigned and only does routine flybys. At this time of year, still feeling the tug of migration, she is away, soaring more. With the letting up of the hawk's torment, Mis becomes more confident. But I still worry. Despite her rapidly increasing size, she is very young and fragile.

Each lunch hour, at the peak of the sun's warmth, I walk with my flock of dogs to the orchard. On the way we detour to wild single apple trees, in search of booty. The fallen apples are cidery now and make capital toys. Eye-rolling dogs swagger around with apples bursting in their mouths, looking like the proverbial boar's head. First they play with their plunder and then they eat it. I sit on the round bare rocks and watch while they tilt and contest over the grave of our former dog, Grog. Sometimes the older corgis play with each other, and Savannah even reverts to the crazy circling of her youth, or they bask, brief hind legs stretched behind them. Often they rebuke one another and herd. In a few short weeks Missy and Rose have become the best of friends, and on these excursions they play endlessly at a ritualized kind of Elizabethan round dance. The dry grass blows, and I can almost feel the pleasure of it for dog feet.

⌒

It is at about this time that the lessons that I have been learning through Merak about the harshness of nature come closer to home for me. One morning when I return from driving Jeremy out to catch his school bus, I am startled to see a small corpse of a beautiful rust color stretched near a mullein plant in our front dooryard. The likely cause of death for this pitiful lean-bodied young fox is all too plain—porcupine quills—not a lot, just enough in the mouth and a few on the front paws to make life a lethal hell. I think back to the tortured mewing last night, at which the dogs had been frenzied. Then I had supposed the noise had been that of a female porcupine, and I had reeled the dogs in hastily and shut the door on the night. But now I can't help wondering whether the fox had not come to us for help in the extremity of its suffering. For, when I help Barry put the body in a garbage bag for removal to a safe burying place, through the plastic it is still warm and limp. What can I think but that she waited the night, hoping for the last, remotest possibility of help.

I remember how Grog dreaded and always avoided the car except on the many occasions when he was quilled. Then he immediately headed straight for it and the trip to the equally dreaded vet, who he nonetheless knew to be his only hope of help. It was

110

surely too late for help by the time the fox appeared, but I grieve
also because this must have been one of the bright cubs that Barry
and Morgan had watched play in summer. And now it is stretched
in a cruel, wasted death. Later this morning it does not really
help much when, reading a book on birds of prey for details
about Merak, I am reminded that nature deliberately provides
an excess that is expendable.

Turning from this small tragedy, I set myself to hang clothes. I
am nearly to the socks when Bird feathers by softly, competently,
and I have the impression that she is remarking to me, "You've
got to see this!" She ends with the scrabble up the barn's steel
roof that she now only does if she's too self-satisfied to bother
with accuracy. I am surprised by her cheerfulness, because at
seven-thirty this morning we had shouted back and forth like
fishwives over her cruelty to baby Mis, but then I see an amazing
thing. A foreign hawk has followed her closely and now circles
her head a couple of times. How will Merak take this flagrant
and unprecedented intrusion into her territory? Proudly, she shifts
feet, and I begin to be suspicious. The flight silhouette of the bird
which dares to approach so close to Merak appears quite different from hers. The intruder has a longer, barred brown tail and
slighter, shorter wings, and is generally smaller. Surely it cannot
be another red-tail. Yet I remember that immature hawks can be
surprisingly dissimilar in appearance to their mature form. Far
from being discouraged by our hawk, the stranger performs odd,
giddy loops over the clothesline, while Merak shifts easily to get
a better view. Within a quarter of an hour, the skittish newcomer
moves toward the ridge's thermals, leaving Bird to fly directly to
the leafy top of a nearby elm sapling, where she lands neatly and

peers out coyly from the leaves. When I hurry in to check a field guide, my suspicion is confirmed. Merak's companion is an immature red-tail.

No one knows for sure why female red-tails are larger than males. One theory I like, suggested by ornithologist Tom Cade, is that limited available food supply in the nesting territory has led males to adapt by concentrating on small prey while females focus on larger quarries. The male feeds its small catches to the female and young early in nesting season; once the nestlings are large, the female hunts as well.

Another theory has it that small, fleet prey is more common and is more easily caught by a smaller hawk. Since at times the male must provide for the entire family, his smaller size would be advantageous. Furthermore, as I have learned from observing Merak, there is no doubt that egg production, even more than nest building, is stressful for females. Some experts suggest that females may need to be larger so they can accumulate reserves in order to produce their eggs.

Although my hopes were high that Merak would join up with the young hawk and through him become more wild, he never reappeared, possibly because he was too young to be seriously interested.

On a Sunday, after a week when wet snow lies on the leaves and bitter raw winds blow, the clouds are swept away, leaving a mildness in their place. Merak has been getting a mouse to bolster her during the cold spell, and today she takes it to gulp on the logs that seal the old farm ice storage chamber. Mis astonishes me by sauntering right up to the hawk. I am beginning to see that wolfhounds have long memories and that Mis is not prepared to forgive Bird for all the tormenting when she was younger. There is a maniacal glint in her eye as she cocks her head and peers wickedly at the hawk, who is flabbergasted by this insolence. Luckily, Merak is in her best mood and preens and postures for at least twenty minutes before she gets bored, flaps up, cruises Missy, and scrapes up the nearby barn roof to her roost.

As a teenager, our bewitching wolfhound, Missy, is out of kilter. Her hind end is higher than her front. When straight, her long, thin tail hangs to the ground. Already, at just over four months, she weighs sixty pounds. Quite often she looks around over her shoulder at herself in surprise. Her ill-behaved, gangly legs give her special trouble, and she frequently stares at them in bewilderment. The growing, she explains, has just happened; she had nothing to do with it. She is loving and, because she's naturally placid and wants to please, is generally easier to train than Rose. There is, however, a shadow of a stubborn streak lurking in the background. At present, though, she's woolly, vague, and happy-go-lucky. She tips her head up and grins from ear to ear when she plays with the other dogs at night. (Actually, she gestures with her head far more than the Cardigans do, reminding me of the tilts and turns of Merak, or an Arabian mare.)

As the young wolfhound matures, I am discovering the remarkable map she has made of her world here. Through her far-seeing eyes, I am beginning to understand how, from her first walk with us, she has had a rare sense of landmark. If there is so much as a fresh piece of bark on the laneway, she knows it instantly and shies until she has examined it. From the second time we take a walk with her, she knows the path's dimensions: before we indicate that there will be a turn, she knows from memory where the turn will be. From her swift, powerful covering of the roughest land, her bounding through forests, I know she has a different way of judging the terrain. And she practices always, loving to cut as close to me as possible, just as she will do when she makes her breathtaking rushes through the closeness of an unfamiliar thicket.

Overnight, by way of a torrent of rain, we have traveled from early September-like weather to a true November day of hard, clear air and roaring wind, bare trees, and a new, almost birdless, silence. It is a cold both bracing and repelling. When we walk back through the field to the orchard, the dogs are in their element. Rosie, just allowed out for walks after healing a gash in her foot, rushes in crazy circles, whisking through the tall, sere grass. Inspired by her, Savannah sheds her years and joins the younger dog. The wolfhound is fully equal to them both. With open-mouthed laughter and a swaying, whipping tail, she is thundering and heaving every which way in an ecstasy of play, while Annie bobs and rebukes the insubordinate trio with gusto. When the older corgis tire, Missy reverts to ferocious, exuberant play with Rosie. In play, each is studying her specialty. Rose herds, flinging her lithe little body fearlessly at the wolfhound's great neck to steer her. Mis cavorts, paws splayed, leaping and pouncing, ready to lunge down on her prey's neck.

So joyous is the rush of wind, field grass, and dogs that Merak joins in, with a superb display of her flying. She performs a ragged, confident flapping, cutting angles and mastering the difficult and unpredictable wind. This back field, where the dogs and I have had such shelter and happiness this fall, is her field most of all. At last she lands on a tree at the "gateway" to Elizabeth's trail, right where the troublesome, intrusive pair of red-tails had nested last spring, and surveys her dominion with high satisfaction.

This morning there has been an anthem of the winter birds, including sixteen exotic yellow evening grosbeaks, and surveying them all from the fastness of our cottonwoods is Merak. There is a din of distant, frenzied hunters most mornings this week, but, while I am eating breakfast today, a ghostlike lone doe stands solitary near the barn, looking at us searchingly. Afterwards, I wander over to where the doe had stood. I look at the chestnut grove we planted. At the trees' feet their leaves lie crumpled and ugly, but yes, next year's shiny, fat, tobacco brown buds tip the branches. I give Merak her mice out on the grass, and Rose, getting bolder every day, runs circles around her, barking boisterously. Bird tolerates this for five minutes before she takes off for the cistern cover to finish tearing up her breakfast.

At nine, when we step out for our walk, the hawk is perched on the planter by the front stairs, stripping the lovely, spotted feathers off a still-warm downy woodpecker, its head flash amaryllis red. Surely the woodpecker had been stunned by hitting a window. I'd hate to think Merak would plunder the feeder.

What is it about snow that inspires delight? This is Mis's first snow. She licks it and frolics, and she and Rose fling about joyously. A flock of cedar waxwings passes, their trills sounding like the tingle of Christmas tinsel. When we pass my beloved yellow birch, its curly trunk dark and rich from the recent rains, it seems slighter and more supple than I had remembered. Can it be growing younger as I am growing older?

⌒

Missy's loving displays are very unusual: she does a kind of frenzied kissing where she nibbles softly and tenderly with her lips only, and she nuzzles and blows. When she gets that look in her eyes and approaches, Jeremy knows to get out of the way, as she's sure to kiss him with her wet beard. Today, in the hard bright cold, she is a wild girl. So much is she pestering Annie, flinging her heavy "arms" on her, that I have to tell her to stop. Although she is half crazy with the joy of acting silly, she does stop very well, much to poor Annie's relief.

Soon after Christmas, though, I have to put an end to the lovely prancing games we have been playing. She has always been feather light in her leaps against me. It has been moving to have her stand on her hind legs, her front paws resting lightly on my shoulders, but now, with her great size and growing energy, she is becoming too wild about it. Sadly, I know I will have to tell her "no" before she becomes a danger to me and, more likely, anyone else. Her play is unique, with much prancing and pawing and fawning, and curvetting her head, and only occasional hoarse, eager barks. I miss being part of it, but Morgan knows how to wave his arms like a wolfhound and invite her, and she prances and splays her legs for him.

⌒⌒

When Merak's supply of muskrat dwindles, our friends Art and Wendy come to our rescue. Remembering our needy hawk, they offer us chickens they had planned on discarding after a freezer had stopped functioning. Will Merak accept this new supplement, I wonder, repulsed as I am by the carrion smell of the first thawed carcass? Although she has claimed extreme hunger, when I tip the chicken onto the feeder she reluctantly extends a claw to claim the pale, rank corpse, but dawdles a long while before she consents to neatly pluck the flesh.

And she has need of the extra food: by February 20 she has started nesting again, interrupting her fetching of sticks only during a week of extreme cold. After a brief flirtation with the fifty-gallon drum on the back porch that we use to collect wastepaper, she begins a straggling nest of sticks on the back porch roof. During these early stages of nest work, although prompted by light, Merak appears confused by the spells of deep cold, and will stop work for a week at a time when the temperature plunges and a harsh wind blows.

In mid-March she starts to get renewed amber coloring in her winter-drab hood feathers. Missy catches a glimpse of the hawk through the kitchen window, while Merak is ripping at her chicken. Bird, who is now highly territorial, raises her head, and then raises her hackles—the newly colorful head feathers. I have never seen her do this before, but now she upends her head and neck feathers as a cat might and glares at the wolfhound. From the kitchen safety, Mis boldly exchanges glowers.

In the last week and a half of March the nest-building pace escalates. Usually Merak spends a steady two hours in the early morning and another hour or so in the early afternoon fetching sticks. By the time she brings bark to "finish" the nest she is desultory, spending a couple of hours working hard, then loafing in a nearby tree or disappearing completely for the rest of the day. In other words, her loyalty to her nest is still fractured, changing from intense to nonexistent. She remains very protective of her food, and after her glowers at Missy, we have to close the kitchen curtains before she will feed.

⌒

Near winter's end, for all the love and understanding between us, I've come to realize I will have to quell my wild and woolly hound. Maybe it's the approach of spring, or maybe Missy is distressed because Rose is in heat and behaving strangely, or maybe it's simply teenaged cussedness, but the wolfhound has decided once again to play boisterously with Annie. I have sensed that Annie is upset and I am worried about the damage a hound the size of a small donkey flinging her large legs about might do to the older dog. When I call on her to quit, she gallops up to me and returns to the whirling and leaping up at me that I had put a stop to in January. Now I can see from the devilment in her eyes that in her giddiness she could be a danger to all of us. She could easily knock me flat. With fierce, determined gestures I have never used, I punch her and kick out at her flank, ordering her to stop. In spite of my determination to be obeyed, my unpracticed blows are tentative and puny. And, not surprisingly, Mis ignores them.

But this is a struggle I must win if I am to keep this large, beloved dog. I grab her neck fur with both my hands and hold on. For a few minutes she quiets and, fearing to break her will, I release her. At which she immediately glances over her shoulder to make sure I am watching, and leaps on Annie again. I am determined to gain her respect and I know that I must finish what I have begun. I seize her powerful neck, a neck designed to snap the backs of wolves, and force her to a sitting position, and then a lying one, and I hold her there, watching the fire die out of her wild eyes.

For the rest of the day, I have to wrestle her down a few times more, but she is improving and responding to me, and there's something curiously moving about the bond that is strengthening between us as I work with her.

⁓

On a mild, gusty day, the dogs and I walk out directly after breakfast. When we turn toward the great hill and the waterfall, we see Merak working the winds. She is rather shaky after doing little soaring all winter, but she actually appears to be practicing slants and dips, mounting, tilting precariously, all the while looking certain that she knows exactly what she has to be doing.

After a few minutes of breathtaking beauty, she finds a current and slants quickly out of sight, heading east. Later Elizabeth reports that she has been watching a red-tail performing five miles north of here, but surely this could not have been Merak.

⁓

For a few weeks now there has been a mimic blue jay. Out of the fifteen or so blue jays that flock to our feeder, for some reason one has taken to tormenting poor Merak with a passable imitation of the whiny, infantile calls she most favors. I've watched the hawk when this happens (usually this jay calls from the safety of the plum bushes) and she takes the faker very seriously, studying the bushes earnestly, presumably in search of this annoying other hawk. On my walks I find myself meeting this jay in unlikely places, and although I should know better by now, the calls always confuse me until I realize that no, Merak has not assumed a new deep-woods territory. Instead, I am being mocked by a jay who may be practicing his new voice on me. Later I learn that the blue jay's vocal copying is actually considered to be vocal appropriation rather than mimicry. It is thought that a bird that masters additional calls may improve his ability to attract a mate, both by intimidating rivals and by stimulating females.

⁓

In time, Bird's nesting instinct becomes fiercer. The first egg is exactly on schedule for her, on April 5. She lays a second egg, apparently four days later. I have learned that a usual clutch of eggs for a red-tail is two to three, although the range can vary from one to four, with the number of eggs depending partly on the bird's nutritional status. The two four-inch eggs are oval, finely granulated, without much gloss, and a dull, or dirty white.

Egg laying is often spaced three or more days apart, and the resulting asynchronous hatching means there is considerable size discrepancy between nestlings.

Eggs cool when incubation is interrupted, but because embryos are less sensitive to cold than to heat, this is not usually harmful, and few birds incubate continuously. In fact, as the developing embryo increasingly can generate its own heat, sitting becomes less frequent. Experts believe birds can sense the temperature of their eggs with receptors in their brood patches, and that this helps them to regulate the frequency of their sitting. Although I have never seen Merak do so, birds turn their eggs periodically. The incubation period for red-tails is one month. Once the chicks are hatched, the fledging period lasts forty-five to forty-six days.

⌒

With the unusually cold weather, prey has been less available to Merak than in earlier springs. As before, once the nest reaches its final stages, she becomes completely focused on it, and no longer will hunt. We supplement her food with the last of our cache of muskrats, a few mice from traps, and the remnant chickens, which she loathes, but eats. Once she lays the eggs, her absences from the nest become short, usually no more than five to fifteen minutes.

Located as it is on the back porch roof, the nest is completely exposed to the north and west winds that now are prevalent. There is no shelter of boughs, as there would have been if she had built her nest in one of her pine trees. After the second downpour of unseasonable snow, she shows up on the back porch to beg for food, looking hopelessly draggled and wretched, her breastbone lean, and both Barry and I reluctantly decide we will have to remove her eggs. I wanted to leave her sitting on the two eggs for at least a full week, so she would have a feeling of having accomplished her work, but with the weather and her inability to feed herself, I do not want to push her beyond her limits.

When she sets off on one of her brief flybys of the house, Barry dashes up the ladder and plucks the eggs from their bark-lined nest. Later, while I carefully pierce each end of the dirty, blue-white, slightly marbled eggs and blow out the contents with a straw, I can hear Merak plaintively mourning the theft. The yellow-tinged contents, paler in one egg than the other, dribble into the sink. Could this have been the year the eggs were fertile? I am relieved when the final bubbles of liquid egg splatter in the sink. The emptied eggs feel completely light, embryo-less. I cannot know for sure whether they are infertile without shattering them, and I want to give them to Barry to show to schoolchildren when he tells them about Merak, but the shadow of doubt is very little. Within twenty minutes Merak's distress abates and she flies off to sun herself from the surveillance point of the nearby clothes-line pole. Nesting is over for another season.

⌒

Yesterday afternoon I heard Merak calling from the back field and deliberately stood almost beside her window box to get a feeling of her sailing in directly toward me. I caught my breath as she rushed toward me at a high cruise, entirely sure of herself, but acting as if she had not the least intention of stopping. At the same instant that I was beginning an inward flap myself, she gave a metaphorical flick of the wrist; I felt a rush of air; she set her wings forward once more, and plunked down assuredly on the box. In spite of all the time I've spent Bird watching, she still can leave me speechless with the matchless beauty and responsiveness of her flight.

Then today, in the cold gray of early morning, while gazing up raptly on my way home from a walk, I find her high overhead, not so much soaring as just serenely gliding, smoothly, gently, looking and searching. Lately I've had a new awareness of the keenness of her vision. If she's sitting on a telephone pole, she is able to detect the movement of a mouse in the grass two hundred yards away. She is born to see as much as to fly, and does so superbly with all her being.

While raptors' smell, touch, and taste are poor, their hearing is thought to be highly developed. Where they excel, though, is in their superb vision, the keenest of any living creature. Their eyes, three to eight times stronger than ours, can spot distant objects visible to humans only through binoculars. It has been calculated that on a clear day, when the bird's view is unimpeded by clouds or fog, at 500 feet above ground it can see twenty-seven miles, and at 26,700 feet a staggering two hundred miles. Raptors' very large eyes occupy as much space in their heads as do their brains, and each eye functions very much like a telescope. While birds active in the daytime have color vision (in fact, avian color perception may even surpass our own), night-flying birds are thought to be color-blind.

⌒

By the end of March, the lake's ice has become a raft, no longer moored to the rocky shore. All day the lake is moving, shrugging off its burden of scarred, wind-weathered ice. As it does so, it sings beneath its chains, creaking, moaning, and whinnying as if great mammals leapt and plunged within the lake beneath the ice. Already the shrugging has made sharp cracks, rifts, or fold lines in the icy casing.

Closer to home, there is a tracery of bird tracks on the new fallen snow off the back verandah, graceful, airy, as if twigs had been pressed ever so lightly in the fluff. This morning, Merak is a hawk in a bush. I spy her bulk at the tip of a young elm, the blurring snow sweeping around her. She flies in to complain to me, her dappled breast feathers spread until they're lyre-like instead of closed and cupped. I see bloody matter on her scimitar beak and see blood staining a yellow talon. I slip my finger under her wing as she fusses it about—eider softness and lightness, as light in its way as the cold, late March snow.

And then, for one surprising early April day, the temperature soars into the seventies. Driving to Toronto and back with a friend to pick up her new puppy from the airport, I stare through the ashen haze of the unusual and dreamlike heat at the nightmare that people have let happen, apparently willingly, to their land and their city. At Oshawa, long before we reach Toronto, I conclude that the developments are graveyards for fields and woods, and that the box houses are their tombstones.

I come home at six, bursting with elated disbelief that we actually could have made it through the city's hell and back, and insist on grabbing the last of what here must have been a beautiful spring day by going for a walk with Barry and our flock of dogs. We talk our way back across the still fields to Elizabeth's, and we hunch on the rock while the dogs joust. Finally, slowly and reluctantly we are meandering home, stretching our walk until the last stain of orange sunset has left the sky, when we hear the eerie glee of coyotes in high tilt. They are startlingly close, barely a field's distance away. If, as Indians say, geese are souls speaking to us from above, so are coyotes, but capricious, quixotic ones, the Lokis of the land.

However, there is no time to read the high-pitched bubbling song further. Dreading a confrontation with the wild coyotes, we rush to round our dogs up. Annie and Rosie, we find, have no wish for a fight and are at our heels already. But, hackles raised, hardly knowing what she is doing, foolish Savannah has started across the field. She comes back readily to our urgent calls, perhaps not really wanting the showdown we are denying her. But Missy, the untested wolfhound, snorts and bares her lips. Frantically I call her back to us, rip the belt off my pants, and loop it around her neck. Then slowly, fearfully, we all walk back together across the no longer welcoming field, defeated by the shrill, otherworldly cries.

This morning we feel winded by a three-inch smothering blanket of late snow. Everything is dim and reduced to black and white again. Poor Merak is very dismal and, I think, unwell. Her feathers, especially on her breast, are matted and frozen, and she wheeks and huddles from window box to wastepaper drum, wretched and unable to settle to anything. Meanwhile the dogs, with their usual resiliency, take to the snow as if it were a November novelty. Only Savannah wades; the others prance and caper.

Merak's desperate hunger and poor condition may be explained by Frank Beebe's observation that female red-tails usually stop hunting for themselves fifteen to twenty days before ovulation. Normally, after that time their food would come from their mate. It may also be that one of the reasons a female may not feed herself properly before egg laying is that she has become too heavy to hunt.

Glancing out the writing-room window one morning shortly after the unwelcome snowfall, I get a distinct shock. When I see a bird balancing neatly on the wire linking our house with a utility pole, my quick assumption is that it is Merak. But no, this is by no means Merak's plump, affable shape swaying gently outside my window. It is a hawk of a different size and color altogether. Just slightly larger than a kestrel or sparrow hawk, this handsome slate gray merlin (or pigeon hawk), as it turns out to be, has a look of sharpness and competence that sets it apart from our resident red-tail. The intruder is not actively stalking the blue jays and evening grosbeaks clustered at our feeders, but merely asserting his presence. After resting on the wire for five minutes, he carries his assertion further, cutting audaciously to the back of the barn roof, where I now discover that Merak is perched. I am surprised to find that, uncharacteristically, our hawk is completely oblivious to the intruder. Even when it buzzes her head, she pays no attention, focusing studiedly away from the feeders. Having announced its presence, the merlin flies with swift, powerful strokes back through the field, but remains in a flight line with our feeders.

Now that we and Merak are becoming more accustomed to one another, sharing the wonder of her with Barry's conservation-education classes becomes irresistible. Once a group has gathered on our lawn and is quiet, he calls Bird to him, enticing her with a brandished mouse to come and sit on his arm. There is a hush of awe and some fear as the powerful hawk rushes in, talons out-stretched. Most of the children have never seen a large, free bird up close. While juggling the sometimes impatient hawk on his arm and baiting her with the mouse, Barry explains what human imprinting has meant for Merak. Often the children are convinced that Merak is a pet. It is hard to help them understand that she lives completely free of us, visiting only when she chooses to do so. Generally the hawk is delighted with the attention, far more so than the promise of one extra mouse would warrant. If all is well for her and she spots a school bus in the parking lot, she makes a point of finding business nearby, hoping to be introduced. Once, and only once, when her temper was short, she closed her talons on Barry's arm, and he had to continue as if all were well, grimacing with pain. If she is in a good humor, the children are allowed to approach and stroke her gently. And then, at last, the reward. Barry sends the mouse spinning high, and, in a flash, the great airborne bird flings herself on her back to snatch the airborne prey in her talons, then rights herself before she returns to earth. There is a quick display of mantling on the lawn while she gulps the mouse, and, show over, she withdraws to the trees.

~

On this May morning I scarcely shrug when I find the power off. Instead, I take it as a sign that I am not meant to be working indoors. And so I walk out just as I am, long skirt, bare legs, ridiculous old straw sunhat. At first, slightly guilty about the unearned holiday, I stay close to home, listening to the birds—the flickers and rose-breasted grosbeaks, the wren's fountain of song. I pry in the garden, joyfully discovering the latest upthrusting shoots—lilies, colchicum, bellflower. For a long while I stand basking in the thrum of my honeybees, watching their shadows cross their dooryard board on their way into the hive, their leg baskets laden with pollen of colors too numerous to single out. The surrounding wild cherry blossoms are alive with bees. For the first time this spring I can hear my "bee-loud glade" once again. Now, with the slightest stirring of a breeze, the small cherry petals begin to drift down in confetti-like swirls.

In the beginning I am content to loiter close to home. But

watching the rain of petals makes me want to see the old orchard behind the house, now at the peak of its blossom. After this spring's heavy rains, the half-wild field is still sodden and difficult to walk, especially as I am neither dressed nor shod for rough walking. But the mesmerizing charm of the May morning draws me on. Even before I can hear the bees in the largest of the old apple trees, I can smell the apple blossoms' roselike scent. And indeed, everywhere I walk on this day, the trees' auras are almost tangible.

The air is heavy, fragrant with all the tree blossoms of my world, languorous, weighted down by a searching sun, as yet unscreened by summer leaf-shade. Yet in spite of the unseasonable heat, I decide to continue past the orchard and across the field to a whaleback of rocks that I discovered last autumn. In the heat and sun there is a palpable feeling of growth rushing ahead. The mouse-ear oak leaves are swelling, and the oak trees themselves are sending forth lime green tassels. I slosh through the wet field, past the unnaturally bushy and solitary field pine and, at the field's end, turn into the laneway that leads through a young forest. Here I am discouraged to find flourishing more poison ivy than ever before.

Now set on my course, however, I unroll my socks and, tugging them up my bare legs for protection, walk on. The heat, the last lingering blackflies, the poison ivy to be avoided, and the heavy, wet walking steal away some of the day's charm. For all the spring beauty, though, I feel drawn to continue.

Usually when I reach the whaleback's long stretch of granite, I sit for a while, brooding over the lacy green lichens that halo the pink rocks, but today the searching brightness of approaching noon robs the granite of much of its color. I will not linger here as I had planned to. However, heat-dazed as I am, I feel unable to stop walking. I will just go past the rocks before I turn back, I promise myself. It will be a good chance to see if there might be wild orchids in bloom in the queer gully beyond. Last fall I often thought the place seemed perfect for them. A small pine grove, it has acid soil, sphagnum moss tentacles everywhere, and ground cedar plantations under the pines. But this morning I am disappointed. The only flowers I can find are the slight candles of Canada mayflowers that, in the heavy shade, are still not fully in bloom.

Then, as I kneel on a dense cushion of moss to investigate, there is a burst, followed by a stamping and clattering. A doe plunges away through the trees, her long white tail flashing an alarm. As always, I am rueful that my intrusion has sent the deer off, and sorry also that I have been unable to see her better. Now, I wish I had remained sitting on the rocks. If I had, the deer might slowly have revealed herself to me, unafraid and natural.

Although I have missed my chance with the doe, I am sufficiently aroused by her startling exit to want to keep going. I decide to push on out of the pine thicket and along a well-worn animal trail, which leads to a small, secluded pond. Possibly I might sight the bittern I have heard glunking back that way. Out once again walking in a heavy field and under the breathless sun, not surprisingly, I do not find the bittern. After all, his booming call generally comes in the early evening. Instead, a host of redwings shrill their oka-lees, guarding their nests in the cattails by the pond.

Idly, I follow a chain of rocks extending through clumps of willows into the heart of the pond. Standing at the tip of this rocky peninsula, I bend to pick up a freshly cut maple sapling, its keys still hanging from its branches, and shake my head over the surge of beaver that has led to the recent exploitation of even pitiful little pools such as this.

Suddenly and nearby, I hear a startling, coughing scream. The sound has some of the quality of the howling bark of foxes that scour the fields on moonlit nights. Yet—and there it is again, and then once again—there is a difference. While the fox calls sound utterly ruthless, like a primitive violence howling out of the earth itself, they have always been steady and decisive; they're used to startle prey and to keep in contact while hunting our fields. But in the sounds that I am hearing now, there is a note of panic and uncertainty that is almost a vomit of noise. With a jolt I understand the dangerous proximity of the cries. At the same moment, I see a broad flash of reddish brown. It is the doe, pacing restlessly at the edge of the pine grove. Now I recognize that, by following the deer trail out onto this peninsula, I have effectively cut myself off from escape.

The menacing—and I am beginning to be aware of just how menacing—calls surely are coming from the doe which had dashed past me. Either she is preparing to give birth, or (and far more likely) she is defending newborn fawns that must be hidden in a glade all too near me. In either case I am realizing that the actions of what normally would be a timid, furtive creature, now not only will be totally unpredictable but also may well be dangerous. Except for the first warning flash, I have not even seen my foe. She is there; she is not there. I have only my ears to grope with if I am to know my adversary at all.

The only obvious escape route runs immediately past the deer. It's true that she has retreated to the thicket again, but her howls are increasing in frequency and agitation. Never before on my walks have I let myself get in a position where I could not safely get out. In the midday heat there is an unreal quality that keeps me from confronting the very real danger I am in. The blackbirds continue to sing; nothing has changed except for the doe, who now is silent again. Did I imagine the menace? On such a morning surely nothing dangerous could happen? Is this how a mesmerized rabbit feels when she is confronted with a pursuing fox? My eyes dart, trying to consider possibilities. On three sides I am surrounded by brackish, shrub-filled pond. It would be virtually impossible to swim away from the doe's territory: even if the pond were shallower than it appears, its bottom surely would be too treacherously soft for walking; anyhow, the very thought is disgusting.

But the danger is real; I cannot afford disgust. The deer renews her trumpets. I will have to do something to protect myself right away. Then maybe I can consider how I am going to escape. There are no trees sturdy enough to climb, and even if there were, they would only offer a temporary solution. I have to keep reminding myself that this deer is not simply passing through. She has an urgent need to protect her nursery. Still dazed by heat and disbelief, my first instinctive act is to snatch up a large branch that I could brandish, if necessary. But alas, the only branch that comes to hand is a rotten piece of old fence rail. It might add stature to my waving arms, if I were desperate, but certainly would crumple if I were forced as a last resort to use it against the deer.

And so I stand, profoundly alone, on a morning so beautiful it makes a mockery of the fear and menace confronting me. A strong sense tells me to wait it out. A sneaking wildness within suggests that I would gain from the experience. If I sat quietly on the shore of the pond for a few hours, surely the doe would become calm and go about her business, letting me see her fawns. But a more common sense warns that in this situation time would not help. Sooner or later I must cross that nursery and surely renew the deer's panic.

The increasing bellows, circling closer, tell me that I should be taking the threat seriously. I will have to investigate other escape routes, however difficult they might be. My first thought is a deer trail leading away from the thicket, but down through heavy shrubs into a muddy, wet tunnel that is only waist high. It would be useless: to pass through I would have to crawl, and if the doe were to follow me I would be hopelessly outmatched. Looking from the rocks over the willows and across the pond, I know that beyond the boggy area surrounding me there must lie what I hope will be a safely distant field with a sheltering corridor of tall spruce.

So, drawing on long-forgotten childhood stalking skills, I begin cautiously advancing my feet across the marsh grass from hummock to hummock, sometimes using my rotten fence-rail as a balancing pole, sometimes clinging to the dense marsh shrubs, conscious that if the panicky deer were to attack, I have worsened my position: it would be impossible either to keep my balance or to jump and wave my arms as I had earlier thought of doing. Another howl, closer yet. In order to get beyond the nursery to the open field, while avoiding the turbid water at the pond's center, I discover that I first will have to parallel the doe's grove, actually approaching her territory.

And at long last the phantom appears. Her red sides steamy and heaving, she is stamping and snorting, phlegm flying from her flaring nostrils. An involuntary roar escapes my throat, not of fear, but of challenge: "I am here. I have my own power, and I am standing my ground. I am not attacking, but I am going my way." I swipe futilely at my sweaty face with my arm, and continue my hopping, snatching progress through the swamp, whipped mercilessly by the wiry bushes. My long summer skirt is enough of a hindrance that I seriously consider ripping it off. I am thinking in terms of steps now, with no chance to look up at the redwings circling my head, protesting my intrusion. Each step must be carefully plotted to avoid sinking into a couple of feet of water and oozing, soupy mud. Apparently oblivious to the danger and to my undignified, absurdly slow progress, my mind chatters on: Is there nowhere wild one can walk in May without invading hotly defended territory?

At last I am heading away from the nursery, and before long the next few bellows are quieter. Apparently the deer has receded. Now, perversely, I find I am almost sorry. I have not wanted to distress the doe, but I also do not want to lose touch with her and her riskier world. I have only been seeking sufficient latitude to move beyond the line of her territory. I regret the yell that broke off our encounter. I wanted to win her respect, not to cow her.

Soon, the water becomes shallower, and I hop into a field choked with wiry steeplebush. To my surprise, I find that I am intensely disappointed that the encounter is over. The treacherous question remains in my mind: what if I had walked most slowly and steadily past the doe, avoiding threatening eye contact? Could there have been a middle path, where neither of us gave ground? Alas, I was too civilized to try the experiment. But now I am filled with regret. The still lovely day has lost its edge.

To avoid the densest part of the spruce plantation, I have to veer back one last time toward the far side of the doe's thicket. She is still vigilant, and once again she trumpets. And in the ensuing silence, again I miss the electricity, the reality I felt during our confrontation.

Ahead, I find an opening in the hedgerow that divides the plantation from the orchard field. In the damp mud there I see that this has been the doe's doorway into the orchard, a favorite winter haunt of deer, where most of the past cold days we saw five or more, wandering as in a frieze. Crossing through into the orchard field, I also regret that I have been an intruder, albeit an innocent one, in a world where I plainly have no place. Returned once again to a pastoral, cultivated world, inevitably I have a sense of relief. The difficult walking is over, and survival no longer forces me to pitch my senses high. But there also is sorrow at losing this pitch. The drama back in the pine thicket seemed more pungent and powerful by far than my life at home.

Overhead I discover Merak soaring, tentative, gentle, making sure that I see her, skipping one wingbeat when I gladly call her name. As I so often do, I wish she could share her sightings with me. She surely must have known all along about the doe and her nursery, must have seen the fawn too. And how many other vital things does she see that I will forever miss? As I trudge back to safety, I feel hopelessly distanced from her world.

～

The next day, Jeremy stays home sick with a headache. Relieved by the breathing space from the restrictions of school, once the headache abates, in the afternoon he reverts to last year's home-schooling routine. Happy, self-possessed, he calls the big bird to him and stands for twenty minutes with her on his wrist while she blissfully gaws to him, her favorite person. She tweaks the pocket of his red shirt and admires his watch and his ear, always favorites; she plays with sticks and dandelions and chortles to herself, reminding me of that old-fashioned word "hobbledehoy." In short, she is about as happy and loving as a bird can be. When she tires of playing, she sunbathes, draping herself at full wing on the lawn.

～

After two days of sultry storms and then, yesterday, great winds, overnight the temperature sinks to an unseasonable coolness. This morning brings a hard, gray cold and a wind that is ripping the tender husks and even some of the leaves from the trees. When I hear Merak crying, I look out and find her, midair, in the middle of four large birds, with her feet shot out, warlike. The birds, silhouetted against the dark windy sky, do not form the classic turkey-vulture V. The wind is strong and challenging, but at least one of the birds is a poorer flyer than Merak. At last I understand—this must be the other family of red-tails, with their just-fledged nestling, practicing the winds. Merak must have worked out a rough relationship with the adults—"so far and no farther" on both sides. Today, though, things have become more complex with the introduction of the immature hawk. I now can explain some of her past month's distress by the nearness of the intruding hawks. However, how do I explain today's truce? It seems that more overlay is possible than I had imagined.

Because the state of a bird-of-prey population—its numbers, breeding success, and so on—is dependent upon the availability of food, the number of red-tails hunting our fields suggests an abundance of food. Michael Everett, in *Birds of Prey,* emphasizes that nature normally preserves a balance between the hunter and the hunted. Only in a local territory, or for a short period of time, would a predator eliminate its food supply.

For the next two days, Merak is solitary, and I conjecture that the parents have been staying close to the nest site. Once again I feel pity for our bird. It has been made clear over and over this spring that she is a misfit.

⌒

In the eighty-degree heat of a July afternoon, I bumble over to the garden to do some of the last weeding before we gather the now golden-dry hay for mulch around the plants. As I head for the very back beds where the bean plants are flowering, I am startled to meet Merak fanned out over the zucchini. For a moment I feel a flash of fear that she might be dying, so limp and draggled are her wings. Then I quickly remember how, in the dandelion time of her first spring, she sat beside Jeremy on the grass, wings equally stretched to enjoy the sun. Beak open to pant, every feather reaching out away from her bony body, Bird is merely sunbathing.

Soon after I start work among the beans, she recovers herself sufficiently to strut over to my patch of earth, where she shows me how she can help by tearing up a few plants, and flinging others about. When that pales, as most amusements quickly do for Merak, she undoes both my shoelaces and "kills" them. And then she pounces on and eats a dragonfly, which I can't help thinking must wriggle and tiggle inside her, like the fly celebrated in the song "I Met an Old Woman Who Swallowed a Fly." Eventually, Merak flies off to harass a phoebe in front of the barn. Later, hot and thirsty after clearing a whole row of beds (during which I am pleased to discover that the purple basil has sprouted after all), I head back to the shady coolness of the house for iced tea.

As I pass Merak, as plainly as if the hawk herself had reminded me, I am prompted to think that it is more than time to resurrect her wading pool. Morgan half-fills it with cool water for me, but then uses it to bathe Rosie, who, just returned from a shortcut through the pond mud, has transformed herself into a wholly black Cardigan. However, I have scarcely finished my tea when Barry calls me to watch a hawk who is blissfully bathing once again in her own green plastic wading pool. She sluices and dips and shakes her entire feathery entourage, and draws water into her open, thirsty beak. Although she may know instinctively, as the wild birds do, that a water-laden bird is at a disadvantage, she lets me sit by the pool taking pictures, before she flies serenely, if heavily, to her telephone pole for preening.

⌒

By chance, while we are camping in Vermont, Barry and I discover the Vermont Institute of Natural Science's Raptor Center, in Woodstock. Always searching for a better understanding of Merak, we make a detour to visit it. Even though we arrive at opening time on a breathlessly hot day, the center is filling with visitors, and we have little hope of being able to talk to an official on such short notice. But luck is with us, and a volunteer tells us that if we go up the winding, rock-bordered trail to the care area at the top of the site, a center expert will meet us. When we are introduced to Julie Tracy, who cares for the resident raptors, it is difficult to explain Merak to her—a hawk who plainly is human imprinted, and could be said to be in our possession (a warning flag for anyone who cares about wildlife), and yet lives generally independent of us. She makes it plain that she disapproves of Merak's living free, and that she thinks our red-tail would be better off caged and protected the way her center's birds are. However, in spite of the pressure of a lineup of people forming behind us, she is generous in her time and advice.

She intrigues us by saying that not much is known about human imprinting. Our experiences with Merak may be more valuable than we had imagined. However, her anecdotes are not encouraging. A human-imprinted bald eagle, she recalls, when put in a cage with others which were not, proved to be very anti-social. She warns of the danger that might come to us and our visitors from a human-imprinted bird. She knows of one owl that eventually mated with another. Once it had done so, it began to see people as its enemies, and it became dangerous. A human-imprinted hawk that raised a fertile chick, as Merak someday may do, she cautions, might well turn on her human family in defense of her feathered baby.

I ask a difficult question: How long might we expect our hawk to live? Generally a red-tail's lifespan is seven to eight years in the wild and slightly more than double that in captivity, she tells us. However, while her carelessness might well be against her, Merak's not migrating, her being fed and cared for by us, and her raising eggs are in her favor.

From *The Birder's Handbook* we learn that perhaps as few as 10 percent of birds of prey make it to breeding age, and that most deaths that occur after birds leave the nest are among inexperienced young birds. Though raptors in general are long-lived, eventually most birds die from one of the risks they face each year, rather than from the attrition of growing older. Because they feed high on the food chain, they are susceptible to poisoning by pesticides and other pollutants. Longevity is also closely correlated to size. The larger the species, the longer it is likely to live. The maximum lifetime recorded for a red-tailed hawk in the wild is twenty-one years and six months, but Kit suggests another interesting wrinkle: we may not really know the longevity of wild birds because aluminum bird bands wear out within thirty years.

After we leave Ms. Tracy, we visit the various cages, enjoying peering into their depths to find a variety of hawks and owls as well as eagles. Watching the enthusiastic reactions of the many visitors, we appreciate that it is valuable for people to be able to see and become somewhat familiar with these birds. The cages are ingenious, sensitively devised habitats for birds that would not survive in the wild. There is no more cruelty here than there is in letting Merak take her chances. And yet I come away feeling I have not truly seen a bald eagle, nor a saw-whet owl nor a turkey vulture. If a corpse is striking because it is utterly bereft of life, a creature unable to live fully in the wild surely is robbed of much of life. Seeing these well-cared-for caged birds emphasizes how thoroughly independence feeds vitality.

It is a rare summer day when I have the place to myself and I am panicking for fear of wasting the precious time, so I start by taking the dogs for a walk through a deliciously cool morning. As I go, I chew over the unfamiliar dilemma of how best to spend my free time, used as I am to spending most of it on helping to raise our sons. I've been trying unsuccessfully to decide whether to set aside writing this summer or to continue trying to finish my book.

The walk continues this mood of indecision. And on such an exquisite day, rich in birdsong, vivid with summer flowers—Saint-John's-wort, mullein, daisy fleabane (never have I seen them as lush and tall as they are this rain-blessed summer)—I feel more frustrated by my inability to fall in with the summery holidayishness of it all. Dogs thunder up to me, dogs pursue chipmunks, huffing dogs lag behind, but, just as I can't get inside the beauty, I can't get inside their zest. At last, halfway home, a glistening teardrop of pine sap catches my eye. When I go over to look at it more closely, I become caught up in the strength of the large tree's presence. I stroke and sniff the gumlike older resin, and press my nose against the warm cork of the pine's trunk. Bending round the circumference to follow a pattern in the bark, I come upon a moth's perfect camouflage. Furry of body, clinging to the complex body of the true pine, the secret moth rests; its mottled wings are pine bark to the essence. At last I have a welcome flash of wonder and a reminder that the essential need is for looking deeply and faithfully. Nothing will taste as sweet if I don't remain connected by continuing my writing. I lay my hand on Mis, who has padded up courteously to see what I am looking at, and turn purposefully toward home.

⸺

The wheel of Merak's year rounds once again and, just as she was pulled by nesting and egg laying in spring, now once again the urge to migrate tugs at her. She flocks up with passing turkey vultures, and is more frequently absent. Earthbound, I spend afternoons longingly watching her soaring, fiercely trying to imprint her splendor in me, in fear that I may never see her again. As I watch from among the shining grasses and blowing milkweed seeds, however, I keep my word. Never, by so much as a gesture, do I indicate to her my wish that she never leave.

⸺

After a week of rain, the landscape is of an almost primeval swampiness. The air breathes wetness, and a lurking mist hangs around the roots of things and further dulls the sky. Even when it doesn't rain there is the heavy dripping of past rain and a visible greening of the mosses and lesser roadside plants. Without the softness of their leaves, the trees are stark.

In the afternoon I glance out and see a gang of beagles racing down our laneway, lusting on the heels of a wounded doe. Rushing out, I find that the dogs have brought the deer down at Morgan's pond. She lies there, cooling a shattered hind leg in the water. Oddly, the dogs, having run her down so wildly, do not attack her once the advantage is theirs. Instead, they now hang about her, clambering around the agonized body and licking her gently.

When I return home and call the neighboring hunt club, the men quickly come to make things right and to secure the deer. They are saddened. They know it is wrong that she was left wounded the day before. We agree that she must have plunged onto conservation area land, and must have run for several hours before seeking sanctuary here.

And, oh my heart, the sanctuary has to be denied. There is no place so safe that it cannot be violated. And, after all, what would constitute safety to a deer in mortal pain? All the dogs now are chained, except for a young one that breaks and scampers away when the powerful gun fires. First the hunters shoot several times into the water to drive the doe nearer shore, and then they finish her quickly and take the body away for a crippled friend who hasn't been able to get a deer of his own. Clean, quick, and decent.

Except for Merak, who has witnessed the whole scene. She has flown to the hanging elm, where she has a close view of Morgan's pond and the kill. The strange dogs within her preserve have disturbed her, and the atmosphere of bloodlust followed by the struggle in the water and the violence of the gunshots has upset her to the point where she is screaming wildly. Perhaps it is only fear and distress that her territory has been savagely invaded. And yet I wonder if she isn't trying to protect another wild creature. She hasn't reacted this way when stray dogs or strangers have intruded in the past. As soon as the doe dies, she becomes silent, although the strange men and dogs remain for some time, dragging the body from the bloodied water.

In the afternoon's last light, after the dogs have been loaded into one truck and the doe into another, and after the streaming rain has washed away the blood, Merak flies to the window box and calls me out to her. Apparently she is not wanting food, but only reassurance before the approaching blackness of the night. I stroke her yellow, scaly legs and she kisses my fingers fretfully with her beak.

The following morning the men are back again, reasonable, likeable, and still looking for their lost little dog, genuinely grieving for him. They look rather like their hounds, fever-spent, bewildered, looking bemused at the way this crazy urge had taken them. Although I make no protest at all, as they leave they offer that one of them has yet to even fire a shot.

⁓

After hunting season comes a blissful, if unrealistic, sense of peace and safety within the park. What is left? we asked when leaves and birds were flocking fast away from us. And now we find the answer richer than we might have thought: The deer, most of which have summered deeper in the forest, return to their winter yards here. The wintering birds draw closer to our house and feeders. The newly pared landscape alters in our now accustomed eyes from bleak to beautiful. As we begin to turn inward and indoors, our thoughts rest more on shelter and comfort. A week after the doe's death, I sit in the kitchen bathed in the low afternoon sun, enjoying our little rosemary tree. I recently have brought this native of Greece in out of the cold for the winter; it is seizing all the warmth and sun it can get from the kitchen window and giving off a slight, sharp fragrance each time the forced-air heat blows up from the register beneath it. The tree has been a kitchen god now for at least ten winters, and has become an involuntary bonsai, still a small bush but with trunks of slightly shaggy bark. A few of its autumn-pale blue flowers still cling to it. And so, I now discover, does down; the tree appears to be garnished with milkweed fluff. But when I look more closely

I find that actually this is Merak's down, briskly shaken from her breast this summer during her molt, and caught on the spiky rosemary leaves. Somehow I don't wish to remove this new part of the tree.

⌒

All this short November afternoon I have been sitting by a pond far from home, listening to the ice overtaking the pond. In the dim light, I am held by the stillness of the stark trees, absorbed in the brittle voices of the ice's first tentative advance and retreat over the water. The scene was set a month ago, the trees stripped and stiffened in the cold, the beaver lodge furnished with its accompanying food pile of young branches, but only now does the pond begin to concede a final closure to the encroaching, creaking winter imprisonment. The slightest wind shatters the glassy casing, yet even as I gaze a crinkling skin is re-forming near the edge where I am hunched. I peer through the crazed window. A mottled leopard frog is either imprisoned or sheltered within. From beyond the hills come the muffled hoots of a great horned owl. Reluctantly, and only when the last fiery rind of sun is barred by the pond's surrounding trees, do I rise to leave, returning to the artificial comfort of home.

⌒

December, when it comes, is the coldest December on record, and muskrat, Merak's supplementary winter food, has become difficult to obtain. The market for fur has dipped and Gerry and the other trappers he knows no longer find it worth trapping them. And even if they had been interested, Gerry tells us, there are too many muskrat predators this year, which means that there are few muskrats to be had. We spend a worrisome few days watching our hawk's supply of mice dwindle. In the fierce cold, we have been forced to give her four at a time, but still she remains very thin and miserable. Sometimes, like the largest flake in a blizzard, I see her flap by the window, stalking us like prey. When she lands on our back porch, I go out to stroke her and, touching her, find myself wondering all over again at what suddenly seems so very little. It could be said that a hawk is nothing more than a bundle of loose feathers and a light shell of hollow bone. Only her eyes continue to hold weight. On the worst days she no longer is even insistent, but only palely loitering. When I fumble my hand in her feathered cape and find every detail of her fleshless breast bone, I hurry indoors to thaw another mouse as quickly as possible.

At last, Barry's widespread inquiries pay off: he learns that the husband of a former baby-sitter is still trapping muskrats and has a horde of carcasses stashed behind his house. Barry hurries over and returns with a bulging bag of the disgusting, welcome bodies, and the promise of more all winter.

Because the cold freezes everything so swiftly, we have to keep wrapping up muskrats in plastic bags and bringing them back into our basement to rethaw overnight—horrible, liverish blobs. Only the brown, curved teeth and the shapely flailing tail are reminders of their former muskratness. But, just in time for Christmas, Merak can spend a glorious hour sinking feet and beak into the flesh, after which she returns to her winter chimney roost, where, heavy with food, she is blissfully wreathed in steamy heat.

⁓

December 30 is the coldest night of this record-breaking month. With a heaving wind (it seems that even the wind can't move

143

well in such cold), the night temperature sinks to minus fifty Fahrenheit. As always on such bitter nights, I worry about Merak. No matter how house-ensconced I am, she is a silken cord tying me to the reality outdoors. On the next morning, the last day of this year, I hurry anxiously to bring her the rank, blood-dripping muskrat carcass. I step onto the back verandah, where I call repeatedly through lips that begin to freeze in just those few seconds. She *had* been waiting on the front-porch railing earlier this morning—I saw her through the window. Exasperated, I step stiffly off the verandah, hands now rigidly shaped to the handle of the shopping bag holding the muskrat, and peer around the house wall to try to catch her attention. "Bird, big Bird," I coax. Generally she would rush in, wheeking frantically in response to my call. But now, oddly placid, she remains staring at me from her railing roost, firmly declining my offering.

Having at least attempted to feed the biggest bird of my immediate circle, I bundle on every layer of clothes that will fit and venture out the front door to take a pail of sunflower seeds to the chickadees waiting at the feeder. As I walk out onto the front porch, where Merak is still perched, I have a sense that the hawk wants me to look her way, and so I do—straight into the milky, vacant eye of a dead red squirrel, which she is holding clutched beneath her breast. As usual, my feelings are mixed. I rejoice at Merak's superb pride and the apparent ease she is attaining in capturing her own food, and yet there is the dead squirrel to consider, its handsome tail jutting out from Bird's talons and curving around the railing.

When I return from my hasty trip to the feeder, Merak continues to hold the squirrel, still gripped and uneaten, but now she has it repositioned beneath her breast like an egg. And she is talking. She is almost crooning devotion to this food, this proclamation of her prowess, this dear, dead, warm, furry body so devoid of all its squirrelness, so soon to become hawk. As before when I have seen her standing over her prey, I have an impression that she is cherishing her kill before she eats it, almost as if the distinction between prey and child (part of one's own flesh) is blurred for her. But it really is too cold for philosophy, so, shrugging hastily, I bundle the muskrat carcass back in its bag and return it to the cold cellar floor, between the bushel basket of russet apples and the pots of narcissi waiting to be forced.

Late that same morning, relief from the cold spell comes with sleet, followed by a rain, which, in its turn, becomes a treacherous glaze of freezing rain, coating everything. In the afternoon, Merak sails in to the back verandah, now curious to see whether her current muskrat is available. Her taffeta feathers are crusted with unmelted ice. Although I know this to be a good sign that her heat is guarded within her feathers, when she takes off into the late afternoon dimness, the added weight plainly is a burden for her. What a pity it is that she refuses to roost safe in the shelter of the porch.

Early in January, I am driving home in the last dark light of a gray day, when I am surprised to see a great, blurry shape part with the dead elm at the lane's end. The shape flies slowly westward to the pinewoods surrounding the campground, where I've suspected Bird to be roosting of late. This must be our hawk, although it is almost too dark to be sure. This is much later than she usually retires in winter. The dead elm is Merak's watch tree, her southernmost boundary. Could she have been waiting to make sure I returned home?

Yesterday at sunset, when Barry and I walked back through the fields, I thought of how she sometimes flies from post to post of her territorial trees, and how I felt then that she was our totem, a guardian of sorts. Well, perhaps our human-imprinted hawk is not powerful enough to be a totem, but at least she is an emblem of our territory and clan. Seeing her perched on her elm at the end of our lane when I drive home, as I do tonight, I always feel that I am crossing into a different realm to which her benevolent tolerance gives me the keys.

The next morning, I can hardly finish my bread making for watching Merak and Rose. I don't know how it began, but, when I look out the bathroom window, I see the hawk standing placidly on the frozen lawn. Plainly untroubled by any thought of danger, she cranes her head only enough to keep an eye on Rose. There can be no doubt that, unlikely as it seems, the well-fed red-tail and the corgi are playing together. Rose dashes in circles about Merak, bounding and rushing just as if she were herding the other dogs. Her frenzy is just sufficient to show that this is a game, with none of the dangerous tone a real herding episode would have invoked. Merak, looking well pleased, strikes attitudes that say plainly: "Ha, ha, you still can't catch me. You wouldn't dare." Ten minutes later, a bored Merak calmly flaps up and away in a hawk-version of a saunter.

In mid-January, in spite of the cold, the hawk becomes unusually independent. She is "So-what?" aloof about muskrats, when Barry calls her. For a change, he takes from a mousetrap a fresh, warm mouse corpse and lays it in Merak's back-verandah window box. As he says, she is the only red-tailed hawk trained to appear at the sound of a mousetrap's snap. Lately, however, she has scarcely bothered to present herself even for this delicacy. Since her breastbone feels well covered, I surmise that she has been feeding herself. Perhaps she has caught one of the rabbits in the lane, whose numbers are at the peak of their cycle.

This morning brings a sudden burst of warmth, prelude to tomorrow's promised rain. There is a hazy, warm sun, air tangible with a breath of snow, and, as we return from our walk, Merak in a distant dead elm, utterly at peace and indifferent to us. Just now, she is as nearly independent as she has ever been, but I wonder what another month will bring, when she feels tugged by the urge to breed.

⌒

It would be hard not to believe in fecundity, a quivering like the spring music in *Carmina Burana,* when the weather is so utterly and unexpectedly beatific. I can't remember another end of January when the fields were bare. Yesterday, Sunday, we saw two, then three, then five, and at last six deer in the orchard, browsing, as tranquil as cattle or Bach's sheep that may safely graze. Because we lingered watching them, they set the tone of the day, one of those rare days when all is lovely and easy. A sweet wind is blowing in. How could I have forgotten how sweet the wind can be?

Later this day (although it is only January 24) while at my workroom window, I keep noticing Merak flouncing about among the small bushes in the hollow just before the old orchard. She performs a lot of ridiculous tail waggling as well. It has been such a springlike day, I really can't blame her for the foolish behavior. But I have to keep reminding myself that the spring she apparently is anticipating could be months away. I should also have reminded Bird, because at noon she shows up on the back verandah at the window box, her window box, with a modest nest-twig.

⌒

Two days later, after streaming rain and a shrieking south wind, the morning is cool again, though still windy. Last night, hearing limbs torn from the cottonwoods, I kept waking to worry about Merak. But this morning, here she is again, as sure of herself as ever, merely annoyed because I have designated today as a fast-day from muskrat. All the morning she makes free with her land. At noon, when the dogs and I blow back through the fields for a walk, I discover that she does go farther from her home territory in winter than I had thought. She is soaring in brief bursts, apparently working only the steering tips of her wings, then landing in different trees, as if trying them all, and then soaring again. When the dogs and I reach Bachelor Beaver's Pond, I catch sight of her far away to the east, skipping over the distant Lost Pond. She almost certainly didn't roam so far last winter.

Today for some reason the jays have gathered in the spruce plantation, with their usual noisy talk. Savannah, hearing their fuss, doesn't even bother with her usual foray in search of rabbits. On our way back home, when we reach the barn field, the two rock doves who come each day are now flapping fussily about the barn, clearly doubting that this is the right sort of place for them at all. And indeed, in all the years we have lived here, this is the first time that doves have come. Their beauty makes me muse about cutting a heart-shaped hole in the top of the barn wall, under the eaves, and keeping white doves to fly around. Merak continues to lead me to all sorts of strange thoughts, chief among them a wish for increased intimacy with other birds.

Watching the assurance with which our hawk now takes the air or lands on the shakiest of trees, I think that the clumsiness of her first years was not for nothing. Rather it was symptomatic of a long, risky childhood. Her casual, unplanned, and gauche movements at that time now seem like an extensive testing of her limits. Eventually her many mistakes gave her a certainty of recovery from any predicament. Now, even in the gustiest of winds, her control is superb, as is her technique for landing on swaying wires or spindly bushes. Do other hawks take so long to perfect themselves, or has she been slow in maturing because she was seized prematurely as a nestling?

～

At the end of January, I wake in the stiff, early morning and cannot fall back to sleep. Merak did not come round at all yesterday. As the day went on I tried unsuccessfully not to think, tried not to consider all the possible ends that might befall a still slightly infantile red-tailed hawk. I pushed from my mind the thought that she might have been smashed by a branch in Saturday night's gale-force winds, or that she might have idled on the ground, as she sometimes does, and been seized by a predator. Or had we given her something too rank for her to eat, something that had spoiled too drastically in the recent warm weather?

Once again I am surprised by the depth of my distress that she is not within our skies. I try not to think of how hopeful I recently have been for her, seeing her superb, sure flying and landing. I try not to think of her starting on a new nest, or how we have been looking forward to seeing whether she might find a mate. In short, I try not to think of how her story might have ended too soon.

I hurry Barry downstairs for breakfast and am delighted to discover a chastened Bird sitting on the front of the barn roof. I rush to the basement to fetch the muskrat I have been thawing for her and then hasten out to hold it up to show her. Perhaps she has been absent because she found food of her own yesterday. If so, she will not bother with our offering of carrion. Generally, after she has killed something, she basks in our trees, indifferent to us. Now, however, she squalls at me and I begin to wonder.

At first she refuses to come to the window box, and when she does she is flighty and nervous, jumping even when a chickadee rushes past her to snatch a seed from the nearby feeder. I begin to wonder whether she has been hiding from something that has frightened her. Could it be that the recent warm temperatures, which had persuaded Merak to begin her nest a month ahead of time, have drawn another red-tail back here early? Is what I am seeing now a reflection of her frustration at being powerless again to defend her territory?

Then, only minutes after her fretful appearance, in the still grayness she is gone again, and we are waiting for a small snowfall promised for the early afternoon. It seems that, with her return after her unexplained absence, we can look forward to the next chapter in Bird's story after all.

❧

Once again, by mid-February Merak has been around less, but she seems assured. She is also uninterested in our food, so we assume she is well. She adds a second large stick to the back-porch window box, and, as the nesting impulse strengthens, she becomes moody: gentle and loving one moment, querulous the next, screaming from the barn roof but flatly refusing to come to the porch when we are there. I have to suspect she is flying considerable distances beyond her territory these days. Generally, if the dogs and I walk back through the field, she is vaguely present, just asserting her right to be there, flapping her way from the apple trees to the ash trees along the fence border, and then to a clump of sumacs at the back of the field. Yesterday morning she was nowhere to be seen.

❧

We take advantage of a brisk, March-like day of wind, sun, cold, and almost no snow to go for an exuberant mile-long walk to the very back pond of the park. While there, we explore the isthmus of land between Bachelor Beaver's Pond and Back Pond, an area of strange old trees and gullies that I had never visited before. Without ever admitting it to Barry, part of my purpose in walking back this way is the hope that Merak might reveal where she has been lurking. But she never appears, or, if she does, she never lets us know. Only when we dally back toward Elizabeth's house in the late afternoon sun does she show up to perch in her favorite—the biggest—of the apple trees.

A month later Merak is still confused about the ideal spot for her new nest, having spent a few days trying in succession the front porch, the back verandah and the flower box. At last she settles on the gently sloping back-verandah roof, a site we think is preferable to her other choices. The last few days have been full of soupy mud, seeping water, and wraiths of fog that blow in and out. Merak has become very clear and certain. Far busier than usual, red tail flashing, wings spread, she has been sailing and flapping near the house, plucking branches from an assortment of trees, the catalpa being a favorite, or strutting audibly on the roof. Merak's performance has improved with practice. Not only is a ratty pile of heavy, budded cottonwood branches accumulating on the sloping verandah roof, but also I am watching the hawk grooming the shingles with her beak, evidently thinking she can make them a part of her nest.

Observing has proved more difficult this year. Bird has become more professional in her nest building. Her effort this spring is well formed—the edges are built up higher than in previous years. This means that we no longer can see into it, either from Morgan's window above or from ground level. The only way to check if and when her eggs appear is to climb up a stepladder and crawl across the sloping roof.

What with the muddy ooze and broody females, this feels like an achy, restless time. A few weeks ago I watched Rosie, now fully mature and in season, rolling her eyes, groaning softly, and dragging herself around, swollen and heavy with hunger for mating, and now I watch Merak, flopping and swooning her wings over her precious sticks and keening her baby talk to herself. Our hawk has been begging for extra affection from Barry and me, and this is not sexual, I think, but, rather, as was Rosie's before, a soliciting, in her bewilderment, of help from all her tribe.

⁓

Soon we are forced awake at six by hearing our trees alive with redwings, more than we ever have heard before. So urgent and triumphant is their singing that it thrusts its way in, even through the window Barry hastily closes. But this morning I am too excited to return to sleep. Kit is sending two immature male redtails for release in the park today, and we are all hoping that one of them might mate with Merak.

The morning blooms into a dreamy, too hot day (even a shirt feels too hot, after months of heavy coats) filled with returns and reappearances, so many we can barely keep up with them. The bees are dancing outside their hive. Right after breakfast I take a supplementary bucket of syrup down to help them get started, and their activity lures me into standing for twenty minutes, watching. It takes me that long to be convinced that I really am seeing pollen on their legs in what still appears to me to be a pollen-less world. Strings of wild geese fly over while I loiter at the beehive. I hear the pure, lovely call of song sparrows, and see mourning cloak butterflies, freshly emerged from hibernation. The mourning doves have returned here again, and robins are busy everywhere.

When an Avian Care "ambulance driver" arrives with the boxes containing the young hawks, we walk over with her to release them beyond our barn, while two bluebirds warble to us from the overhead hydroelectric line. The first hawk is timid. He hunches in his cardboard carrying box and doesn't utter a word of protest when Barry gently draws him out. Unlike Merak when she first came out of her cardboard box, after only the slightest glance around, he takes off in a low, wavering line, away, as far as possible, from us, the box, our house, and habitation.

Immediately interested, Merak interrupts her nest building to fly to the barn roof and inspect our activity. Her scream is not unkind. The second male then erupts from his box, hissing bravely. By now prepared, Merak takes to the air at exactly the same time the second male does, and the two cross paths in midair, as he heads for an elm in the nearby swamp, and she flies to a closer elm, one of her territorial trees. Although she appears superbly unconcerned, we can see that there is not one second when she is not fully aware of the released male bird. Over the whole afternoon we, as humans, can find nothing to fault in Merak's performance. Far from screaming menacingly as she had when the mature pair encroached on her territory last spring, she begins by ostentatiously turning her back on the male, spreading her wonderful tail and slightly puffing out her already superior size. But perhaps to another hawk, her performance is unconvincing. As surely as the pair had been instantly aware, from a distance and in a flash, that they were male and female, had he recognized the infantile flaw in our poor bird? For an hour he stands his ground in the swamp. Although we no longer can see him, Merak, nest forgotten, flies across the field to a second elm on higher ground and waits there for nearly two more hours, preening and displaying herself, evidently conscious that the male still is within her territory.

Then our hope must be abandoned as Merak returns disheartened to the house, too dispirited even to trifle with her nest. Perhaps the shock of being freed on an exquisite spring day after a winter healing in captivity has overwhelmed the immature male; he has to establish himself in his world before he can think of mating. Perhaps he simply isn't mature enough. Two days later, as Merak returns philosophically to her plucking of trees, I cherish a small hope that one of the males might remember her and return.

❦

Red-tail pairs are monogamous and devoted, remaining mated for life in successful habitats, which makes Merak's inability to secure a mate all the more sad. By as early as February, courtship displays may be well underway. During these courtship flights, John Terres describes the male as flying as high as one thousand feet, and being able to see a breathtaking forty miles. These displays are much more demonstrative and spectacular in regions such as ours, where the hawks usually are migratory, than they would be in regions where pairs winter. They may consist of undulating flights, and the female's rolling over in the air and presentation of opened feet. Sometimes the two birds actually lock their feet and whirl briefly earthward before breaking apart to continue soaring. Having read of the smaller male touching the larger female's back lightly with his talons as part of the ritual, I wonder whether the very light brushes Merak sometimes makes when she passes by us are a way of relating to us, her tribe, rather than an act of aggression.

～

Meanwhile, a surfeit of longing continues to fill these spring days. First there was the moaning and brooding of Merak and Rose. Now Mis, too, is in heat, confused and off-color, grinning furiously at all of us. Even the maple sap, rushing up into the freshly crimsoned upper branches, wells from the lower gray trunks.

There has never been more of a sense of wings about the house than now, when I look up to see Bird brushing by and around and over the house, a slanted wing, a shadow, a flash of large feathered motion. We are surrounded, as if with a protective veil, by our great, strange bird.

～

Our muskrat supply now exhausted, we are having difficulty obtaining mice to supplement Merak's currently very inadequate hunting. When the Avian Care volunteer delivered the red-tail males for release, she warned us that Kit was having difficulty finding sufficient mice even for her own charges. Was this a message that hard-pressed Kit, always so generous in supplying us, could not bring herself to deliver?

Finally, Barry puts his foot down: "Merak can hunt perfectly well. There's no reason why she should still be depending on us. In April, when it warms up, we'll cut her off completely, at least until next winter." I am shocked by the rebellion mounting within me. I truly fear for Merak, who might well know how to hunt, but so often seems to be too immature to do so. But she does hunt better now, and is rarely underfed. I am forced to admit that I want to maintain the contact and the special relationship

155

with her. This is simply yet another letting go for me. All the same, I dread the thought that we may have to watch her sicken from lack of food.

Now comes a most March-ish day, which begins with iron skies and the slightest flurry of snow. A harsh northwest wind rips the clouds into fleece and brings an enamel blue sky. But alas, the gusting wind also strips Bird's poor heap of sticks from the back-porch roof. She comes around each day pleading for the food I now must restrict to every second day. I stroke her lightly, cupping my hands over the warm curves of her feathers, testing her well-being, prodding her fluffed-up breast, and I can see that all is well with her. Nevertheless, I miss the feeding almost as keenly as she does.

When I let the dogs out at eleven, I see two red-tails taking the gusts. They are too distant for me to be able to tell whether Merak is one, but it seems unlikely. Although there is very little doubt that she will be able to hunt for herself this year, I never have heard her make the harsh, lovely keer, the hunting call I now hear coming from the wild red-tails overhead.

The next day starts grim and flinty cold, which only relents ever so slightly by late afternoon, when the sky clears and the sun, at least, becomes warm. At four-thirty I slip out to refill the back-verandah sunflower seed feeder and meet up with Merak. Desperate for food, she flies in to her former window-box-cum-muskrat-feeder, screaming and doing her most frantic, insistent, hiccuping sort of talk. Keenly sorry for her, but unable to help, I walk to the back of the verandah to look westward up the hill to the pines, watching the first sunset colors. Soon, if not already, difficult-to-see Mercury will be visible in that quarter. I am touched to my core by the sweet, cool purity of the sparrows' evening songs. The cold is so harsh it soon will drive me in, but as I breathe in the rare, bell-clear northern air, I feel in every atom of my body that this broad, lonely land of piercing vision is profoundly home for me.

Merak, having given up on me as a source of rescue, quiets. Aware of the approaching gusty, dark, cold night, and grieved by my inability to help her, I move my hands over her hunched and folded wings, as if scenting her wellness, testing her strength and will to make it through the night and on through the long, chill spring. Sensing nothing out of common, except perhaps a little more lightness than usual, I fall into a broody, unwise kind of love. Completely off my guard, I press my cheek against her face, perilously near her rapacious beak, and fondle her scaly yellow feet, indeed finger each flake of her, now in love and not in testing. Now, without the patron/benefactor role, with me standing beside her in the searching, buffeting wind, as helpless as she to ease her destiny, our understanding seems to clear and deepen. At last I step back and the great bird draws her wings up and out and beats steadily, faithful unto her being, off toward the deepest western pinewoods and the falling night.

⌒

It has been raining for five days, drizzles and dribbles and gales and gusts of rain. Everything is sodden, and color is reduced to various heavy shades of dripping brown. The unusually deep frosts from last December still haven't left the ground, which heaves and twists, in some places leaving hand-deep cavities and earthy frost crystals like a secret ice coral underlying the land.

Merak's pain and distress is obvious. She begs continually for food, although I reluctantly have stepped up her rations. She is alarmingly thin of breastbone again, and, what is worse, seems to have lost the waterproofing on her belly.

She still flaps between nest sites. This week the place of choice has been the oil drum two-thirds full of wastepaper on the back porch. She teeters on the rim, or clambers in, recklessly scrunching her tail and angling wings, squalling incessantly, plucking haphazardly at old cracker boxes.

I've decided I have to increase her feeding, at least while the weather is so cold and wet and while she is going through the stress of egg production. We have had a windfall of mice, so I can keep her going until at least mid-May. Art and Wendy had been hoarding mice caught in their barn to feed their resident northern shrike, but it has flown off north now. Hearing of Merak's plight, they passed on their pail of frozen mice to Barry. It might have made an interesting experiment to pursue nonfeeding, regardless of the consequences. Perhaps she could survive. But my curiosity isn't strong enough to experiment with her life. We'll try again to wean her in that lull between nesting and molting.

The most promising note in the current annals of Merak is that we have not discovered any evidence of raccoons raiding our compost and wastepaper cans. If she does lay an egg in her new garbage-can nest, it may be safer than were the exposed eggs on the front porch. As my mother has pointed out, we can't know that her eggs will not be fertile this year, since there has been so much activity with passing and released red-tails.

Under a cold north wind, but sun and cloud, too, the dogs and I pull off the protective winter leaf covering from the flower beds. In the crumbly soil beneath the leaves, I find so many old friends, the splendidly spotted pulmonaria, doing extremely well, the bushy lavender, and the chartreuse feverfew. A scent of bergamot pervades two different gardens, although its new shoots are barely detectable. Merak surveys us from overhead. I wouldn't know she is there except for the shadow circling my feet as I carry baskets of leaves off into the field, or for a wind-rush from a wing brushing my cheek. That same afternoon, I return to admire the clear beds, fresh canvas for the fruits of my work, and see that the strength of the sun has drawn up inch-long shoots in just this span of time.

Alas, Merak's trouble continues. At last she may have managed to attract a male. Unfortunately, he flies too guardedly for us to tell if he is banded, which would have suggested one of Kit's releases. For the past week, she has flapped between being our baby and his. She cries continually, flounces over to us, running along the ground, apparently seeking assurance that she is one of us, then spies him in a treetop and soars off, crying to his silence. The other night the two of them soared a duet into the haze of the setting sun. The male has been here every day, but only part of each day. But the pair seem attached in a way I cannot sufficiently understand. When they circle, it is as if there were an invisible bond between them.

To guard her nest, she has taken to roosting near the house, most likely in the cottonwoods. One night at bedtime, when I turned on the verandah light to call in our barking dogs, she flew wheeking to the window box, but then of course was not able to return back out into the dark night. Now, she knows not to come if the light is turned on, but mutters hoarsely from the nearby trees if we turn on the light or go out at night. This past week, whether inspired by her other hawk or because wild food is plentiful, she has hunted completely on her own, including catching a rabbit on the park road near the campground.

The first week in April, Merak lays her first egg, and, four days later, a second one. After leaving her to brood them for a week, her condition and the rough weather persuade Barry to raid the nest. I check the eggs carefully, confirming that they are indeed once again infertile. However, where in the past two years she has quickly regained her independent life, this year she continues first to inspect the wastepaper drum, then her roof-top nest, where she still spends time. Was the egg-sitting period we allowed her too short?

On April 20 she starts testing the garbage can and fussing over her porch nest again. Around April 30 we discover that she must have laid a third egg. Because she refuses to leave the nest, even to eat, Barry and Morgan remove the egg on the evening of May 3. This time, perhaps because they have to steal the egg while she is on the nest, she is highly upset. The next day she flies at the bedroom window screen when she sees Barry inside. He calls her with a mouse, trying to ready her for a class, and she does come, but is difficult. She continues to linger around the nest, to the point where we wonder whether we may have to destroy it in hopes of distracting her. Of course, it may be that her instinct is too strong to be broken artificially. How many eggs can she lay?

Almost as if she suspected our intentions, she now decides that her back-porch-roof nest is unsafe, but her options are ridiculous. Worst, and most common, are her attempts to set up house in the north-facing eaves trough. Only slightly better are the sticks she lays out for the wind to blow away on the peaked-roof gable of my writing room. These alternatives are high enough and awkward enough that we would have real difficulty checking and perhaps removing a further egg. Is there any use removing it? How long might she sit if we didn't? How might we keep her sufficiently fed if she sits as long as instinct dictates? She is temperamental and difficult, and highly changeable.

On May 11, Merak is at last released from the thrall of nesting, mating, and defending her realm from the red-tail pair, which, as last spring, now have gone farther afield. I see her painting the air hers, dipping, looping, and soaring, marking every particle once more. Another egg-laying session and its fruitless results has passed.

⌒

Early in the morning, a phone call comes out of the blue: "Is there anyone at your house who would like to go flying? Can she be ready in twenty minutes?" My new friend, Bill MacLean, who has heard how I long to see the park from a hawk's perspective, is calling.

Within nineteen breathless minutes I am at the tiny, sheltered airfield, with its runway rushing out to the lake. Waiting for me, Bill already has his Piper Cherokee 140C out of its hangar. "It's just about a perfect morning, I think, clear and still and mild. We should do well."

Always fascinated by airplanes and flying, as a girl I used to race around Toronto International Airport's elevated parking lot following the great airships as they floated down runways, leaping in spirit at the heady rush of takeoffs and landings. Later, I relished every chance to fly, first in large planes, and then in smaller, domestic ones. As I have grown older, I have felt an increasing wish, while flying, to come closer, and still closer to the earth. I have gazed wistfully at the small planes that cruise over the park, crying inwardly, "Take me too. Please take me too." This will be the smallest plane in which I have flown, and the first time I have been seated in a plane's cockpit.

Bill shows me his great care in checking his flying machine. His attention is unfailing; his fingers are wise. So fine a teacher is he that each step of the process becomes clear, simple, and elegant to me. Likely because he is no longer young, I sense an infectious awareness of risk, and the sharp respect it commands.

He goes back to the hangar to fetch a pump to fill the front tire, and then we step up on the wing, swing into the confines of the cockpit, and seal ourselves in with door and seatbelt. The wall of dials before my nose comes alive as Bill turns the key. In very few words he explains the various indicators, and we decide to check the altimeter as we rise over the park, so I will know definitely how far above sea level I live. As he swings the plane around I have time to begin, only just, to reflect on the very different and complex considerations demanded by human celestial navigation.

Before us is the very faint blur of the propeller. There is the liftoff. We are bereft of land. Being and becoming airborne are very different. In the real effort of lifting the plane's weight, we are climbing hand over fist into the sky. This wished-for venture nonetheless is frightening at first. I find it difficult to get balance, to adjust to a different, flattened plane of vision, and a changing one. I am distracted by the very close quarters, which could be said to be either snug or cramped, and the odd dome of the front window immediately before my face. I feel I have lost too many of my normal bearings—and yet, as Bill reminds me, in a gigantic reach of faith Charles Lindbergh flew the Atlantic with his main fuel tank obscuring *his* front window. Distracting, too, is the clumsy-feeling apparatus with which one rises (or barges) into the sky—grinding motor, the powerful vibration. Being airborne feels so odd, I keep saying to myself, so odd.

But then, just before we reach the lake, we cross a sweet June field spread with masses of pink clover. I begin to find my bearings, to physically realize that I am dealing with three dimensions. Our movement is along three axes, longitudinal, lateral, and vertical. We became airborne in a rush time, swifter than thought, but now time slows.

Bill does relatively tight turns over "The Mountain," until I begin to see the land there as a series of lagoonlike beaver ponds. I notice the queer flattening of mountain and trivializing of rock, that I have seen in aerial photographs. Cattle have become the size of my finger. Would Merak see with relatively similar reductions in depth and scale, or does she have superior compensating mechanisms? We see where the old Pinecrest Lodge burned down, and we study the quality of soil in the freshly seeded fields, admiring the Taggarts' careful stewardship. I wonder about the apparent lessening of the algae buildup in the lakes this spring, but we agree that with this spring's unseasonable coolness, growth may well be two weeks late. I experience another odd leap of perspective when I crane to glance directly below me and see a tiny shadow plane, our companion, swimming to the right of us along the ground.

The flight turns out to be a fine experience for understanding Merak, for it becomes a flight of thermals, of seeing clouds being born. Even after our early morning start, when we fly along the ridge, the bumps from the thermals are noticeable. By the time we cross over Sand Lake, Bill proposes that we come back to earth early, because he doesn't like the way a freshening wind and turbulence from the rising air bubbles are affecting control. Summer heat backup, he calls it.

Then, starting down, I have the best experience of all, what Bill respectfully calls "coming to an understanding of the ways of the air." Because the breeze has become so difficult, he has to circle twice over the town and Sand Lake, trying to feel the wind sufficiently to get his landing just right, and ends by having to approach from the south of the tree-lined runway, the way he considers dangerous.

Too quickly, the door is unlatched, and my feet cross the wing and are on earth again. Swiftly, silently, we winch the plane back into her dark hangar and secure the doors against the bright day. And then I am home again, as if I never had been in the sky at all.

I am left thinking of the complexity and subtlety with which birds adjust to flight. An airplane is an artifice, a flying machine; a bird is art. All day I am mildly drunk with the ecstasy of flight and the glimpse of its technical challenges Bill has seeded in me. But if I've been "wingy" myself ever since, I've also been curious to find out more about how Merak becomes airborne.

Everything about her has been designed for flight. Evolution has pared her weight to the minimum, her bones are strong but light, and, to reduce weight, her reproductive organs almost disappear outside the breeding season. Her heart is large, her lungs have a remarkable power for oxygen absorption, and her body temperature is high for rapid combustion of fuel. When I return to the boys' battered volumes of *The Audubon Society Nature Encyclopedia,* I read: "[A bird's] whole feathered structure is bound together by a beautiful design of membranes, muscles, and sinews that swings each feather through its proper positions to function throughout the thousand split-second changes of a wingbeat." Confronted with the weight and pressure of air, our hawk must lift and carry herself forward through the air with the least possible disturbance. Her streamlined shape fits itself into the natural lines that the air follows in flowing around it.

But when I think back over the pleasures of the day, what most symbolizes flight for me is Merak's serenity when all is going well for her. Her eye becomes mild; she talks chuckishly to herself. Her flight then is truly like rowing.

⌒

This year a silly pair of phoebes has ill-advisedly chosen for their pretty, moss-lined nest a site just left of the back verandah door. When they showed up early this spring, we didn't welcome them. Barry objected that such nests attract extra mosquitoes to the crowd that blackens the porch-door screen of an evening; I have never liked the aggressive and raspy territorial "phoebe call" of the birds. However, it appears we have no choice. The pair is determined to use our verandah.

As the month continues, we are won over by the gentleness of the birds (once they were established, the "phoebing" ceased) and by the rare prettiness of their nest, a delicate mossy cup which took days of effort to create. When at last the first demure beaks peer over the cup's edge, we are disarmed and prepared to like the phoebe children.

Always, with verandah nests, we worry that our cats will catch a nestling prematurely; so, when we deem the birds are fitting too precariously in their nest, we usually confine the cats for a few days until the babies are safely fledged. Although the infants are almost visibly larger each day, thanks to the parents' tireless pur-veyance of glassy-winged dragonflies, we thought they would be safe for another few days. Yesterday, to the deep distress of the phoebe pair, Merak sat for a long half hour on the planter log by the verandah steps enjoying her power to annoy simply by her presence. And Merak, in her turn, also was harassed. Glancing out the back door, Morgan saw Small's paw shoot out from the porch lattice next to the planter log, and boldly whack, whack, whack at the hawk's tempting tail feathers.

But the phoebes are not the only birds disturbed by our hawk's presence. Yesterday afternoon, the blue jays returned with their first batch of young, apparently to introduce them to our feeder location. For an hour, Merak and the jays exchanged insults, something that would never happen in the winter, when Merak and the wilder birds all feed peaceably in the same range.

The air is heavy with an evil, vaporous haze this June morning. Just after I finish feeding the dogs, Merak arrives at the back verandah squawking crossly for mice. Because her breastbone has been alarmingly prominent this past week, and because she is now well started into her molt (I found a first discarded flight feather under the cottonwoods two nights ago), I've been giving her extra feeding. There can be no legitimate reason for this early morning demand; most likely she simply is cross with the miserable morning and her molting. I ignore her and turn to stir the porridge on the stove when I hear a particularly challenging gaw. Glancing over at the window box I see her arch her head upwards, staring speculatively at—oh horrors—I realize her intentions. Infuriated by the weather, her molting discomfort, and the lack of immediate forthcoming mice, she squalls at me warningly, then, making sure I am watching, flies directly at the phoebe nest. Her talons outstretched, she slashes the nest off the wall, tumbling the barely feathered babies to the porch floor. Already it is far too late to stop her as she now has torn the nest from its safety in the very upper back corner of the verandah and pounced on two fat feathered babies, crooning sweetly to the writhing wings until the beating stops and the ripping can begin. Still watching me with an angry triumph, she gobbles first one baby and then another.

To those bearing witness in the kitchen, there is a mixture of horror, frustration, sorrow, resignation, and enthusiasm (on the part of the dogs). Naturally, the two younger cats suggest that they are obliged to hurry out in case this is something they should be involved in. Breakfast becomes an unpleasant affair. Morgan announces that he now hates Merak, that she is making life impossible for the other birds and creatures—just look at the way she once again drove the orioles away earlier this spring. Jeremy points out that in his opinion the dogs are equally troublesome, and that his old friend Bird at least is an authentic wild animal and not a cosseted pet. Barry vainly tries to impose some harmony by emphasizing that this bitter little triumph for Merak is only a part of nature.

Viperish Bird. At this point, I am compelled to dash out with Jeremy to catch his schoolbus. It seems kinder to the infant phoebes to let Bird finish her carnage as swiftly as possible, so I simply leave in haste.

When I return from driving Jeremy to the bus for his last day of school, Morgan pops out the front door: could I come in for a moment before I take the dogs for their walk? He has something to show me. While I have been away, he has returned to the scene of destruction and has found that there are four remaining babies trapped among the gardening paraphernalia of tools on the verandah. These he has lovingly (I hadn't realized how close to the surface ran his old vulnerable, loving side) tucked in an apple basket, shrouded with paper towels.

Remembering former biology student Sinbee's long-ago rescue of swallow babies, I suggest to Morgan that he put the shredded nest remnants into a cottage-cheese container. Then I help him snuggle the limp babies in the moss and consider how to make the nest safe and acceptable to the phoebe parents. All we can think of is to nail the cup to the verandah wall where the old nest had been. And this works well. Morgan leaves for his summer job much happier.

Now, however, at ten o'clock, I am left with some questions.

Merak returned half an hour ago to rake around, quite vocally, her verandah-roof nest sticks, directly above the restored phoebe nest. Will she leave the survivors alone, or is this the beginning of a return attack? For that matter, what prompted the unprecedented first attack? While it is possible that she has learned to raid nests for baby birds as do other birds of prey, I think it is more likely that this was a peevish territorial maneuver.

Quite simply, this morning she resented the phoebes' intrusion on her porch. For weeks, though, she had tolerated them good-naturedly, enjoying teasing the parents by perching on the flower-container log at the edge of the porch but never showing the least interest in the growing babies. Come to think of it, I wonder if her attacks on my houseplants, now summering at their peril on the back porch, are prompted by her territorial jealousy. The other remaining question is a mounting doubt as to whether the parent phoebes will accept a cottage-cheese container nest. So far they have sat only on the clothesline and phone wires, chirping grievously.

There follows a period of anxious waiting. It takes the gentle, foolish birds most of the day to cease their distressed scolding on the nearby wire and return to their children. But the hawk never does approach the nest cup again. The four remaining babies, whom we barely dare to observe for fear of fatally distressing their parents, wax fat and, at the appointed time, fall and flap out of their nest and into a wide world, where a seemingly benign hawk resides.

⌒

Once we reach midsummer, and Merak has regrown all her new, oily, glossy, dark feathers, except for those on her head, she finally has learned to hunt for herself. We often see her in her usual survey spots. Occasionally she comes begging a mouse, or in the very hot weather urges me to refill her swimming pool, but she also is silent and apparently away for two or three days at a time. In spite of her new independence, she remains determinedly territorial about her place here; Jeremy saw her drive off an osprey at noon the other day. She continues to become more accomplished as she gets older.

Meanwhile, on July 4, after taking Jeremy down to town to catch his ride to Kingston for his archaeological volunteer work, I take the dogs for an early walk. If I had forgotten that today Mis is the Birthday Dog, she emerges from the flowery road verges to remind me, garlanded with blue and yellow petals that have caught in her soft, curling aura of fur.

On this anniversary of Missy's arrival I find it hard to remember all the trouble we had with her when she was a baby. This year she is a superb, full-grown wolfhound. She is affectionate, playful, and generally obedient, although she still has an unfortunate streak of what wolfhound breeder Mary Morrison calls "wolfhound deafness."

First Fanny the skunk, and then Merak and now Missy, the three of our creatures who have most closely preserved a wild streak, have displayed an unpleasant, tormenting sense of humor at times when their lives suited them. Missy, with her long ancestral memory, crouches, chin and stomach to the ground, haunches tensed, for as much as ten minutes, with only an evil gleam in her eyes to show she's alive, luring an unsuspecting corgi close to her, before exploding at the dog in a wild burst of flailing paws and tossing neck.

Today, though, she is radiant, leaping up the hill into my vision in her greatness, with her wheaten hair haloed by the glistening sun.

It is the end of October. At sunrise, bluebirds and a multitude of sparrows check to see whether we have set up the winter bird feeder. By nightfall, the first scout blue jays and chickadees join them. Within minutes of Barry's tamping the feeder into the ground, the jays are announcing its return from the nearby trees. Now that we are without leaves again, I have regained the immense view from the bedroom. Newly revealed lake vistas glint through bare trees everywhere. At the northern edge of our horizon, where the white pines march across the Canadian Shield, Merak is waiting. Once again she will be with us over the winter.

⌒

In early winter I forget the nightly routine of bringing in the muskrat carcass to rethaw overnight in its plastic bag. The next morning, Merak arrives promptly at seven-thirty in a mist of fine snow. But alas, her muskrat still is frozen. From her window box vantage point, she watches the dogs rush cheerily into the house to get their breakfast. Staring through the kitchen window from her cold outdoor post, she fluffs her feathers, but still manages to look thin. She must know from the gusts she feels when the door opens, that the kitchen is a tropical paradise of heat and light, of all comforts. (The dogs are now crunching serenely on their food. Barry sets out with fork and can to feed the cats.)

Still hunched waiting for the muskrat that will take several hours yet to thaw she sees the animals polish off the last crumbs. Small canters around the kitchen, vaulting nimbly over chairs. The dogs begin a blissful morning scrap, wrangling merrily over a favorite old bone. But in the heart of winter, there is no play for Merak.

However, a dim satisfaction may be possible. She flies thoughtfully to the cottonwoods near the feeder. Here she whiles away the morning by irritating the blue jays, who continue to feed but also must scold, as they flash from tree to feeder.

～

Tonight Barry calls me out into the muffled cloudy night to hear a great horned owl actually hooting from our cottonwoods. Close up, the soft fluting thunder is shocking. What will the presence of this new intruder mean for Merak?

And then, in the dark before sleep, I start thinking of my need to protect. I am especially anxious at present to keep Morgan safe. How great a struggle it has been to protect a sensitive baby and boy from undue hurt. Soon he will be leaving for several months in Europe, and next fall he will go away to university. Now, after eighteen years of having his care forever close to me, I'm having to teach myself to adopt a new distance. My bright and shiny firstborn has traveled beyond my power to help him much.

The long and difficult process of letting him go forward without my protection is making me aware that something has been wrong with my thinking. I was brought up to believe that if my interests didn't succeed it was because I hadn't tried hard enough. The trouble is, things often have not worked out no matter how hard I have tried, so according to that train of thought, I have to be either a bad, or an unfavored person. My best efforts have never been good enough to move these mountains.

The following morning, I wander back through the fields to the newest beaver pond to think this through. With the wisdom of daylight I recognize that, because I so rarely have questioned my own parents' wisdom, there is one possibility that I have failed to consider—that this way of thinking is unreasonable. My task now is to learn that I can't completely control my own or anyone else's safety—not Morgan's, nor Jeremy's, nor Merak's.

Indeed, I must stop trying. But, with a sudden illuminating flood of warmth and peace, I make a new discovery. This abandonment of inappropriate struggle leads to a sensation of unconditional love like that given to a child by a parent, like that given by God to every fiber of this world. Now, as I try to learn to shed wrongly assumed responsibilities, I shall be strengthened by a feeling of warm arms lovingly supporting me. I sink down onto the rocks overlooking the pond, free simply to listen to the nuthatch in a nearby butternut tree and to stroke the mosses, frozen but newly green from winter rains.

On February 9, once again Merak has started a nest on the back verandah roof. This time it is superimposed on last year's sticks, which rather surprisingly have survived the autumn winds. By mid-February she labors over her nest every day. This year she is more experienced and the nest is a work of art.

Her feathers, assailed by parasites over the winter, are ragged, and she takes advantage of any thaw to take a puddle bath in even the slightest, muddiest pool of water.

The first time the coyotes sing, their cries pierce keen, cruel, and relentless through the moon-filled February night. And then trail into eloquent silence. The next night, the moon is veiled by wisps of swift-flowing clouds. Four times they call—high-pitched calls that spill across the fields, tumble over hummocks and rush into our bedroom—joyous, inviting, and insistent. A kill? A summons to a feast? At last the name "coyote" makes sense to me. "Coy," they are calling, "kaiiiiiiii"—a vaulting, flailing cry that streams over the air like smoke. It is impossible that a sound so compelling, so vital, can disappear, can die to nothing in the air.

By afternoon of the next day I am drawn out-of-doors to see whether I can discover and read more from the night-runners' tracks. In an ambling, leisurely way, I plan to cover a wide oval within the region of last night's sounds. Crossing the nearest field and entering the oak woods near the first of a string of beaver ponds, then doubling back closer to home, will give me two chances of finding prints.

But so mild is the afternoon, so gentle and warm the sun, that I loiter as a deer might, soaking in the sun and the mist off the snow, absorbing the rumble of rushing water under the snow. As I walk on a deer winter runway, I come to appreciate the language of different deer prints. I move past the prancing, pixie-light steps of last summer's fawns and the ponderous, heavyset marks of the aged bucks. Set before my feet are sauntering tracks, leaping tracks, and, later, the drag marks of a deer with a wounded leg. Each discovery illumines the next. All the while, every step I my-self am taking rings out: "This is utterly right. This is what you were made for."

For a long time I pause, looking reverently at one of the largest oaks I've ever seen. At first I can only see the oak as old, sick, and beleaguered. I lean against its trunk, scraping at gypsy moth egg cases nestled in its wounds. But, as my fingers work, my eyes are pulled up into its magnificent, outreaching tangle of arms. Sun and snow mist haloes the soaring oak.

Even if I cannot find the coyote tracks I'm searching for, I am charmed by how much I can learn. The thaw has enticed many creatures to activity, so I find fresh tracks of running squirrels and firm-stepping raccoons. There are mouse tunnels shrinking in the sun and blurry, cross-shaped prints of a grouse long past. Even the language of tracks is fused in time. There is such an ob-vious difference in their ages. The new are crystal formed in ice, while the old are dulled and muted. Walking closely with the snow's text, I am becoming its scribe as surely as if I had mingled with the flesh of the footprints' makers.

The sun is flooding low through the lyre-branched trees now and I am beginning to make my loop back toward home when, almost by accident, I see first one, and then several, large, dog-style prints. I set off beside the tracks as they point down toward what once was the pond of this now-abandoned farm. Hurrying, I push on through thick snow and then out onto the beaver pond's slush. These are the tracks of only a pair of coyotes, which surprises me, since the night cries had sounded like many. One has feet a third larger than the other. The set of the nails in the tracks shows that the pair had been heading toward the pond. Even in the sagging snow I can see that they were moving slowly, and then striding rather than running.

By this point I myself have settled into a rambling, loose-hipped, going-all-day kind of saunter. Crossing the thawing pond, my feet grow very wet, but I simply don't care. Far beyond the pond now, I stumble on through heavy snow, tracking the coyotes up an old deer runway to a far-seeing east-facing ridge. The tracks stretch off, continuing into the great, wild distance that travels beyond the ridge, but, reluctantly, I must turn back. Less than an hour of sunlight remains to help me find my way home.

However, backtracking turns out to be unexpectedly difficult. When seen in reverse, the direction of my footprints doesn't make sense. In my excitement at following the trail, I had been heedless of my inevitable need to return. I had skipped about in order to avoid marring the wolf prints, and so my own trail is confused and irrational. Moreover, so warm has been the day that these uncertain prints have dissolved even during the short time I have spent across the pond. When I regain the point where I first discovered the coyote tracks, and begin to trace their journey back toward the edge of the field, I am disappointed to find that their trail disappears over a large patch of bare grass and black-green moss.

I am nearly ready to give up when I find blurred, apparently older tracks scrambling around a five-foot rock face. Intrigued, I climb around the hill in which the rock is set and find the ground here clustered with coyote tracks, which lead me to the top of the rock. Below me are three back-to-back forms pressed in the snow—the deer must have been lying together here.

In a flash, the story is clear to me. Perhaps a couple of days ago these tracks had been made (after I first heard the coyotes' hunting cries). In the silence following the cries, the pack had been stalking the top of the rock, hovering over the sleeping deer, and then had leapt down to pounce on one. The two coyotes I had followed back to the ridge had been later arrivals, summoned by the joyful cries of the second night. When I had first come upon their tracks, they must have been leaving the prey, sated. There had been no fresh deer prints near their paw marks, nor any sign that their heavy-footed walking had been hurried or especially purposeful.

I spin around, and there in the heart of a thicket, cathedral light is streaming through the bare branches and also through the twisted, wracked, half-bared body of the killed deer. Farther in the woods is a drag of hair, a cast-out liver, and farther still are the entrails, neatly rejected. The deer's head is perfect, a young buck's, sockets as yet unhealed from recently shedding its autumn antlers, eyes staring. His exquisite legs stretch as if still leaping across death, hooves soot black, cloven, limp somehow. It must have been the belly and not the intact, immaculate tan throat that the teeth had prized. It was the belly that had been wrenched open. See how teeth have scraped the ribs lean. There remains only a canvas stretcher of reddened membrane and, seen in a flood of late-slanting light, a luminous chamber. Within the cave there is no heart, no stomach; all is empty. Yet the cavern is humming, strumming. The profound emptiness of the cave reverberates like the chants of Tibetan monks. In the persevering cold of the darkening forest, the body still appears to live. Except for the unlit eye and torn-off tongue, so far it is only maimed, still awaiting tonight's feast.

Long afterwards, and in some ways not so long, desultorily tracing some further convergent tracks, I find my way out of the woods, lost in the idea that I have found more life in this corpse than in the living.

⌒

Tommy Mulville comes to fix the washing machine and go over the latest news about the local deer. After we go pretty thoroughly into the bucks he saw fighting in the back field one night just before Christmas, he stands at the open porch door with me, admiring Merak, who is lurking in the cottonwoods. Unfortunately, the hawk spots Small, who is glowering at Tommy's feet in the open porch doorway, and blitzes the porch railing, intending war on the cat. Tommy, who hadn't noticed Small, thinks the savage flight is aimed at him and is thoroughly startled to see a hawk whizzing in at him, talons outstretched. Having accomplished more than she set out to, Merak then breezes past to resume her nest work, bark whiskers protruding from her beak.

⌒

It is April and I am finding letters from Merak everywhere. Just now her shadow sweeps over me, rapid as a passing cloud. It ripples through the leafless trees and scuds over the bleached field grasses. Over on the hydroelectric line, tree swallows are tipping and chirruping. Only one of them is silent. From her mouth dangles a white, slightly curved feather as long as her body, undoubtedly one of Merak's. This year, her loss of feathers is more casual and random than it has been in the past. Even when the bird is absent, there are reminders of her. For a second year the mimic blue jay is mocking her screeches.

Merak has come through nesting well this year. Her verandah-roof nest, building on the one she had started the previous spring, has been by far her most creditable. She lays two infertile eggs and is able to brood on them for over a week. She proves to be an excellent, responsible mother, hanging around devotedly, spending her nights and nearly all of her day on the nest, as usual disregarding the discomforts of rain or even snow and the possible danger of nights unprotected by trees. With no mate to spell her, and harassed by the frequent disturbances of so public a nest, she becomes haggard. There seems no point in continuing with what must be infertile eggs. (There has been no sign of a male red-tail around, and indeed, what sensible, self-respecting male would become entangled with a female who proposed such an unhawklike nesting site?) One Sunday, pitying her incessant, fruitless, and possibly risky mothering, I tempt her away with a mouse and Barry dashes up the stepladder and confiscates the eggs, which I later empty and save. Plainly relieved by the removal of her charges, Merak takes her loss philosophically. She spends the rest of the morning soaring idly in the sky—a sight we have missed over her long nest building and egg sitting—and she has not returned seriously to the nest since.

⌒

On my way to pick rhubarb in the vegetable garden, I hear a horrific hissing, which turns out to be a baby groundhog, engaged in a futile face-to-face fight with Merak. Each time she sallies up to it, it hisses ferociously, which startles her into retreat. Gradually it backs cautiously into the shoulder-high grass bordering the garden. This leads me to wonder whether she would be able to kill our cats, at least in head-on combat. Perhaps her hunting successes depend on surprise.

Merak is five years old, and the circle is rounding again. It is May, and when we drag the hose over to the garden to water the newly sown carrot and lettuce seedlings, Merak is delighted to come too. More zealously than ever, she plays her snake game with the hose. Wings upraised and outspread, she rushes across the grass, leaping and feinting, pouncing and snatching at the coiling, trailing snake of a hose. The more we laugh, the more she looks to us for approval and the wilder her efforts become, until the vegetables are in danger of remaining unwatered.

Once again we have reached the easy time in the round of Merak's year. A time for lazing and play. I feel a rush of gratitude for having had this experience, difficult as it so often has been. Living with our half-wild hawk, we have learned more than I would have believed possible. Most moving have been the flashes of insight into how it must feel to be a hawk. What remains unknown is whether she ever will fully integrate with other hawks and become truly wild again. Each year she has grown in independence; this spring it appears that she finally, in her own time, has learned to hunt for herself completely. I have deeply appreciated the opportunity to discover that our human-imprinted hawk does become more accomplished as she gets older. Now she is five, but still learning. Perhaps there can be a gray zone between being human imprinted and being entirely independent, and perhaps it is from this zone of indefinite limits that she is emerging.

Unfortunately, this most recent infertile-egg-laying fiasco suggests that that final wildness of mating and rearing young will be denied to her. It seems instead that we should be content with our friend the hawk, enjoying these sunlit moments, and sharing her care when she needs help.

For all her new independence, this morning when I am hanging washing, I hear her incensed screams, warning of an intruder, and locate a pair of hawks working the distant cornfield. A minute later she sails in, lands at my feet, and then actually climbs on my shoe, and once again picks open the lace. I pet her, and tell her she is a fine, capable bird, but she remains unconvinced.

⁓

On a brilliant, exceptionally hot day, I take my lunch, a plate of fresh asparagus and potato salad, out to eat under the cottonwoods. Missy lies beside me, and overhead the hawk rests in one of the trees, plainly at peace. In spite of the beauty of all the flowering trees around me, I am tired and confused after a morning wrestling with writing that had a mind of its own. Rose runs over and jumps up beside me: "Let's go! Let's go!" But I pet her absently and shoo her away. The air is heavy with the perfume of apple blossoms and lilacs, and is drifting with insects and falling petals. A light breeze shivers the fragile new leaves on the cottonwoods, and Merak rises from her perch and flaps off—I assume she is changing roosts from the tree to the telephone pole down in the field.

But once she is over the field, her wing beats become more powerful. I tip my head to watch as, with profound assurance, she ascends the sky, beating her way up a spiral ladder nearly to the zenith.

But then, just before she would have become a dot and disappeared, I discover a second large bird moving toward her, echoing her own dreamy certainty. My first thought is that Merak never would allow such proximity with another hawk. Earlier this morning she was squawking and scolding at every passerby in feathers. This must be a turkey vulture, one of the only other birds she would ever accept at all. But no, the new hawk swings to ride a gust of high wind, proving both by the use of his wings and his fanned rusty tail that he is another red-tail. And now I see that this flight may be more than companionable. Merak glides until she appears to be within wingtip touch of the other hawk. Then the two slip into complete synchronicity and, as a pair, sail together, wheeling now closer, now farther apart, but always mysteriously connected, covering the whole brilliant dome of the sky with their circles. This is no ecstatic courtship flight of wild erratic dips and swirls, and yet there surely is a profound understanding between the hawks.

Now I rise in awe, tears spilling down my cheeks, and stretch my upturned face to the sky, watching the radiant flight, the most beautiful thing I have ever seen, as the two birds move closer and closer to the sun, until, two specks, they vanish beyond my sight.

⌣

Last autumn, Merak enjoyed being called by Barry to show herself off to school classes, but this spring she has seemed too wild and too well fed to bother. Because she hunts for herself, she doesn't need his proffered mouse, and declines to come to his arm or behave properly with a group. For the first time we find we cannot predict when she will appear to us. Reluctantly I am learning that I have to go on faith that she is well from day to day, without being able to verify it. Always, I must be mindful that soon she may never be with me again.

Since I planted our porch flower box early in May, she has

hunted entirely independently. When we see her, her crop is generally swelled to at least golf ball size, and her talons are bloodied. One midsummer day I catch sight of her at the edge of the woods, perched only five feet high and in a sapling. There is a feeling of roundness to her. Her downy head, rounded on her beautifully plumaged body, is snugly encircled within the tree branches. All is most well with her this morning.

This summer, for the first time I've been aware of a rare, strong bond Merak shares with me—not love, but something equally close. After our week's holiday, she made a point of coming to me in the garden, seemingly simply for the pleasure of my company. Since late August she's been absent all day, but comes every evening apparently just to keep in touch. Surprisingly, in her obvious newfound well-being and lack of neediness, she seems more able to be attached to us than when she was dependent.

She completed most of her molting late this year, not appearing with new plumage until mid-August, and even then her head feathers still were not replaced. I have noticed that the crows were also late molting this year, and wonder if the delay may have been caused by unusually low light levels. The hawk's new plumage is uncommonly reddish this year, possibly because of the diet she is providing for herself. There is a reddish glow showing through her darkest feathers and a new, yellowish tone to her breast.

At the end of August, Barry is surprised to find her in a tree deep in the woods, near a beaver pond where he is laboring to repair a badly leaking abandoned dam. So far so good, merely another instance of her appearing in unlikely places. However, then he sees a large, black rat snake basking in a pine tree. We have rarely seen snakes this cold, wet summer, so he leans on his pitchfork and looks at it further, until the hawk lunges recklessly among the dense branches and snatches the snake in her talons. At this point, without thinking, Barry tests her tameness to the full, prying the snake from her grasp. So angry is she that he doubts he will be forgiven, at least on this day. But that night she appears as usual to report at the house and allows him to stroke her mottled breast.

In September, I meet her sitting privately on the campground wooden gate, staring at a tree. Glad to see her, I am drawn to approach and stroke her. She accepts the attention politely, but distractedly, and a moment later I see that my greeting must have been an intrusion. There is a cheep and a rush, and a chipmunk snakes up a nearby pine tree. The hawk has been picking off the campground chipmunks, and I have unthinkingly interrupted her. At this moment I am forced to realize that at last I must start to let her go, at least unless she comes to me at the house.

That same afternoon, I catch the distant, assured keer of a hunting red-tail. I crane my head and see one hawk, circling very high over the barn and making the call. There is no way of knowing whether the calling bird is Merak. Even if I use binoculars I would be unable to see her band. Then I detect a second hawk, rising up the rim of the sky, making swift flaps and testing glides, searching for a choice thermal. Now the first bird is circling closer, too. Its silhouette, with a longer, thinner tail, is unlike Merak's. It continues to call strongly and decisively, and then waits. At last the second, lower hawk moves directly overhead and utters shaky, half-formed keers. These cries sound like the speech of a deaf person. Merak? I ask myself, and almost in answer, the bird dips its head and acknowledges me with her eye, something a wild hawk would not have done. Long after I had given up hoping she would ever learn this cry, inspired by her companion hawk, she is practicing, becoming more accomplished even as I listen.

⌒

I go from miracle to miracle this autumn. A storm is approaching; the air is hot, heavy, and ominous. I walk to the beach, a half hour from our house, and sit watching the waves come in. A gale is blowing up. On the waves there is the glitter of a wan, evil sun. Over my head hovers a large, shadowy bird, magnificently in control of the battling wind. I watch in amazement how able it is to defy the wind with only the slightest tilt of its wings. Merak in this distant place? But so proficient is this bird, and so sure of this foreign territory of ridge and lake, that I doubt the silhouette could be hers. It disappears; it returns; it cuts the wind superbly. It is deftness in the teeth of the approaching storm, giving an exhilarating sense of a creature married to the elements. At last, as if the raging air had become breathless, the bird fans its tail, drops its feet, and sinks precisely onto the top of the wobbly, rotten flagpole, becoming Merak. In her hovering repeatedly directly over my head, she had been present to me, and I have the impression that she wanted me to know how very able she is and how delighting in this other new home of hers.

⌒

It occurs to me that in this drifting autumn weather, Merak, no longer our hawk, is drifting too, in the state between ending and becoming, flying between the realms of death and birth. In limbo, she floats between the secure world near our house and the world where she is a windhover, breasting a gale over lake and ridge. As she moves toward final and complete independence, she is existing in a pocket of other time. Each time I see her, it is a last time. Each time is more a miracle than the last.

Afterword

A decade after I wrote that conclusion, I have found that Merak still comes to us in times of need. It would appear that our house and family remain her center. If this hawk has often tried to step through a door into our particular version of life, we too have been given the unusual opportunity of entering partway through hers.

Each year, though, she is becoming a little less tame. One spring afternoon, as Barry was teaching an admiring cluster of high school students about a hawk's remarkable adaptations, she tightened her grip on his arm. It was only a little that first time, but still it was a warning. At each subsequent performance, learning her power, she clenched sooner and tighter with more of the considerable force of her killing talons. The next year, she refused to fly to him at all. From the security of the kitchen roof, she stood scolding the students she once had delighted in entertaining.

"Do you still have Merak?" is the first question visitors ask. And yes, we say, she still is with us, still flies free. But regretfully, we have to add that she no longer is willing to be present for strangers on any predictable basis. Indeed, in late summer and autumn, once nesting and molting are accomplished, she may disappear from our immediate skies for as much as a month at a time until, one morning, I am glad to see her lurking on a distant snag of a dead elm.

Living with Merak, sometimes I have thought that it may be that all the world now is human imprinted, that is, fixated on humankind's tawdry intimations of what a world might be. And I do grieve for that. Our imprint now is almost universal.

After eleven years with her, it is undeniably apparent to us that Merak's particular web of being is irrevocably damaged. Although most springs she flies out to greet and soar with a passing male red-tail—sometimes even for several days—to the best of our knowledge, union never takes place. Each year, she lavishes weeks on her straggly porch-roof nest of sticks, lays her infertile eggs, tends them, and reaps nothing. By now, we know that it is highly unlikely that she will form that lifelong bond with another hawk, or bring new life to add to the skies.

And it is hard not to see a similar kind of damage in a world where people everywhere speak to me in anguish of beloved rivers that run with poison and of soil that withers. My sometime fear is that the links are already broken in too many ways. The words will barely write themselves on this page, but could it be that the earth is beyond healing?

But always and forever, there is more than one way of seeing. We cannot know what may come to pass. And perhaps learning to live appreciatively with the realities of uncertainty has been Merak's greatest gift to me.

The lessons of living without sure answers offer rich rewards. Since Merak's deviations from normal hawk behavior exclude her from the final privileges of hawkdom—mating and rearing young—there can be no denying that she is damaged. But having said this, I need to add that unexpected benefits have come from these very exclusions.

One of these is that, while Merak seemed to mature to the end of her limits after her early years, she continues to learn and to change. Each year, she finds new and often surprising strategies to expand her possibilities. Also, because she has been afforded the luxury of extended leisure, security, and ease, I wonder whether it can be said that she has pushed the very limits of hawk behavior. She has given me insight into possibilities often denied to wild birds.

I had come to my relationship with her assuming that birds of prey were unlikely to be affectionate. Furthermore, because I was hoping to release her from her human bonding, for a number of years I tried to avoid showing my love to her. And yet, after a while, I started noticing how, if we were away for a week, she showed up promptly to greet us on our return. Although she was always well fed by staff or friends in our absence, it was clear she had missed us and was pleased when we returned. Even if just one of us was gone, she made it plain that she was happier on that one's return. Years after Jeremy disappeared when he left home for university, she is sure to hang around on his rare visits. And only he can be sure of coaxing her up onto his wrist these days.

Of course, it might be argued that what she misses is no more than security. But eventually, when I had given up hope of complete independence for her, I let down my guard. It was then that I discovered how she leans blissfully into my stroking hand and croons to me, how she sometimes grooms my hair with her beak, and how she takes pleasure in my company if I sit by her while she splashes in her pool. Now I know that she is as hungry for affection as any creature I have known, and I only regret that I did not start responding sooner.

Another aspect of her life which may have resulted from her

unusual ease is her sense of play. Freed from the responsibilities of raising fledglings, she has relished games of chase in which she and the dogs alternate as pursuer, or she rushes at window-basking cats, who, delightfully titillated, swear at her from behind the dubious safety of a screen. If no one is available, she gleefully tosses and pounces on sticks for herself, or feints and jabs at the garden hose.

It even appears to me that she may enjoy creativity. Every summer, long after the nesting urge should be ended, from time to time she returns briefly to her nest. As I watch, she putters, adding a few more twigs, stepping back along the roof to admire the artistry of what (to me) still appears to be a messy pile of sticks.

In the end, what I want to say to you is that through the gift of this pitiably damaged yet magnificent hawk I have learned that the lessons of openness in the face of unknowing are available to all of us. What worlds there are in what remains.

Appendix

The order *Falconiformes* includes vultures, hawks, and falcons, which are diurnal (daylight) flesh eaters, most of which have heavy, sharp, hooked bills and strong, curved talons. While most take live prey, some are scavengers. Although the sexes are usually alike, the females are larger than the males. Immature members differ from adults.

Some of the divisions you will find mentioned in this book are:

Accipiters: Medium to small forest-dwelling hawks, which prey on birds. These are strong fliers with comparatively short rounded wings and long tails.

Buteos: Medium-sized to very large soaring hawks with broad wings and fairly short tails. These capture a wide range of prey.

Falcons: Strong, fast fliers with pointed wings and long, slender tails. These eat birds, mammals, and insects.

Harriers: Hawks that have long wings and tails and that eat mice.

Ospreys: Long-winged hawks with a conspicuous crook at the wrist. They hover, then dive for fish.

Vultures: Large, blackish, broad-winged, with naked heads. These are usually scavengers.

Works Consulted

Austing, G. Ronald. *The World of the Red-Tailed Hawk*. New York: J. P. Lippincott, 1964.

Baker, J. A. *The Peregrine*. Harmondsworth, England: Penguin Books, 1970.

Beebe, Frank L. *Hawks, Falcons and Falconry*. Surrey, British Columbia: Hancock House, 1976.

————. *A Falconry Manual*. Surrey, British Columbia: Hancock House, 1984.

Burton, Robert. *How Birds Live*. London: Elsevier-Phaidon, 1975.

Chubb, Kit. *The Avian Ark*. Saskatoon, Saskatchewan: Western Producer Prairie Books, 1991.

Clarkson, Ewan. *In the Shadow of the Falcon*. London: Arrow Books Ltd., 1975.

Coffer, William E. *Spirits of the Sacred Mountains*. New York: Van Nostrand Reinhold, 1978.

Ehrlich, Paul R., David S. Dobkin, and Darryl Wheye. *The Birder's Handbook: A Field Guide to the Natural History of North American Birds*. New York: Fireside, 1988.

Everett, Michael. *Birds of Prey*. New York: G. P. Putnam's Sons, 1975.

Heinrich, Bernd. *One Man's Owl*. Princeton, N.J.: Princeton University Press, 1987.

Kilham, Lawrence, *On Watching Birds*. Chelsea, Vt.: Chelsea Green Publishing Company, 1988.

Kotsiopoulos, George. *The Art and Sport of Falconry*. Chicago: Argonaut, 1969.

Mavrogordato, Jack. *A Hawk for the Bush*. New York: Clarkson N. Potter, Inc., 1973.

National Audubon Society. *The Audubon Society Nature Encyclopedia*. Vol. 2. New York: Curtis Publishing Company Ltd., 1964.

O'Brien, Dan. *The Rites of Autumn*. New York: Anchor Doubleday, 1988.

Robbins, Chandler S., et al. *Birds of North America*. New York: Golden Press, 1983.

Summers, Gerald. *Owned by an Eagle*. London: Collins, 1976.

Teale, Edwin Way. *A Walk Through the Year*. New York: Dodd Mead, 1978.

Terres, John K. *Flashing Wings: The Drama of Bird Flight*. New York: Doubleday and Co., 1968.

———. *The Walking Adventures of a Naturalist*. New York: Hawthorn Books, 1966.

Welty, Joel C. *The Life of Birds*. New York: Alfred A. Knopf, 1963.

White, T. H. *The Goshawk*. New York: Penguin, 1981.

Acknowledgments

First, and most important, are my thanks to Kit and Robin Chubb, of the Avian Care and Research Foundation, both for their care and research of so many birds, and especially for the privilege of sharing Merak's life.

In the same vein, I'd like to pass on my warmest thanks to Elizabeth Campbell of Curams Kennels for Missy and to Barbara Hoffman of Merrymoon Kennels for Rosie.

My gratitude goes to Gerry Mulville, purveyor par excellence of muskrats to starving hawks, and to Art and Wendy Briggs-Jude, of Bluebird Acres, with many thanks for mice and chickens when they were most needed.

Also helpful to this adventure have been: Jeri Harmsen, of the Agnes Etherington Art Centre, for portrait photography; Bill and Ruth MacLean, for my introduction to small plane aviation; and Pam Stuffles, of the Westport and North Crosby Public Library, and Louise Trommer, of the Kingston Public Library, two librarians who went much further than they needed to, helping me search for reference material.

Always, my appreciation goes out to my husband, Barry, for more than any book could express.

For this second, revised edition I also want to thank Milkweed

Editions's Emilie Buchwald and my editors there, Greg Larson and Scott Muskin, for their warmth and understanding. Because of their generous help, Merak's story can be told again, and I go forward heartened and renewed.

PERI PHILLIPS MCQUAY first learned to take joy in nature through the eyes of her Canadian artist parents, Ken Phillips and Marie Cecilia Guard. McQuay and her conservation educator husband, Barry, have been fortunate to live in an eastern Canadian eight-hundred-acre conservation area of forests, ponds, and granite ridges for nearly thirty years. For a large part of this time, she also shared her home with her two sons and a menagerie of wild and domestic animals. Deeply committed to nature, art, and social justice, she is the author of two published books and numerous essays and reviews. She recently completed a first novel and is at work on a second book of nature meditations.

MORE BOOKS ON THE WORLD AS HOME FROM
MILKWEED EDITIONS

To order books or for more information, contact Milkweed at
(800) 520-6455 or visit our website (www.worldashome.org).

BROWN DOG OF THE YAAK:
ESSAYS ON ART AND ACTIVISM
Rick Bass

SWIMMING WITH GIANTS:
MY ENCOUNTERS WITH WHALES, DOLPHINS, AND SEALS
Anne Collet

WRITING THE SACRED INTO THE REAL
Alison Hawthorne Deming

BOUNDARY WATERS:
THE GRACE OF THE WILD
Paul Gruchow

GRASS ROOTS:
THE UNIVERSE OF HOME
Paul Gruchow

THE NECESSITY OF EMPTY PLACES
Paul Gruchow

A SENSE OF THE MORNING:
FIELD NOTES OF A BORN OBSERVER
David Brendan Hopes

TAKING CARE:
THOUGHTS ON STORYTELLING AND BELIEF
William Kittredge

THE BARN AT THE END OF THE WORLD:
THE APPRENTICESHIP OF A QUAKER, BUDDHIST SHEPHERD
Mary Rose O'Reilley

WALKING THE HIGH RIDGE:
LIFE AS FIELD TRIP
Robert Michael Pyle

ECOLOGY OF A CRACKER CHILDHOOD
Janisse Ray

THE DREAM OF THE MARSH WREN:
WRITING AS RECIPROCAL CREATION
Pattiann Rogers

THE COUNTRY OF LANGUAGE
Scott Russell Sanders

OF LANDSCAPE AND LONGING:
FINDING A HOME AT THE WATER'S EDGE
Carolyn Servid

THE BOOK OF THE TONGASS
Edited by Carolyn Servid and Donald Snow

HOMESTEAD
Annick Smith

TESTIMONY:
WRITERS OF THE WEST SPEAK ON BEHALF OF UTAH WILDERNESS
Compiled by Stephen Trimble and Terry Tempest Williams

SHAPED BY WIND AND WATER:
REFLECTIONS OF A NATURALIST
Ann Haymond Zwinger

OTHER BOOKS OF INTEREST TO
THE WORLD AS HOME READER

ESSAYS

ECCENTRIC ISLANDS:
TRAVELS REAL AND IMAGINARY
Bill Holm

THE HEART CAN BE FILLED ANYWHERE ON EARTH
Bill Holm

SHEDDING LIFE:
DISEASE, POLITICS, AND OTHER HUMAN CONDITIONS
Miroslav Holub

CHILDREN'S NOVELS

NO PLACE
Kay Haugaard

THE MONKEY THIEF
Aileen Kilgore Henderson

TREASURE OF PANTHER PEAK
Aileen Kilgore Henderson

THE DOG WITH GOLDEN EYES
Frances Wilbur

CHILDREN'S ANTHOLOGIES

STORIES FROM WHERE WE LIVE—THE NORTH ATLANTIC COAST
Edited by Sara St. Antoine

ANTHOLOGIES

SACRED GROUND:
WRITINGS ABOUT HOME
Edited by Barbara Bonner

URBAN NATURE:
POEMS ABOUT WILDLIFE IN THE CITY
Edited by Laure-Anne Bosselaar

VERSE AND UNIVERSE:
POEMS ABOUT SCIENCE AND MATHEMATICS
Edited by Kurt Brown

POETRY

TURNING OVER THE EARTH
Ralph Black

BOXELDER BUG VARIATIONS
Bill Holm

BUTTERFLY EFFECT
Harry Humes

EATING BREAD AND HONEY
Pattiann Rogers

FIREKEEPER:
NEW AND SELECTED POEMS
Pattiann Rogers

THE WORLD AS HOME, the nonfiction publishing program of Milkweed Editions, is dedicated to exploring our relationship to the natural world. Not espousing any particular environmentalist or political agenda, these books are a forum for distinctive literary writing that not only alerts the reader to vital issues but offers personal testimonies to living harmoniously with other species in urban, rural, and wilderness communities.

MILKWEED EDITIONS publishes with the intention of making a humane impact on society, in the belief that literature is a transformative art uniquely able to convey the essential experiences of the human heart and spirit. To that end, Milkweed publishes distinctive voices of literary merit in handsomely designed, visually dynamic books, exploring the ethical, cultural, and esthetic issues that free societies need continually to address. Milkweed Editions is a not-for-profit press.

JOIN US

Milkweed publishes adult and children's fiction, poetry, and, in its World As Home program, literary nonfiction about the natural world. Milkweed also hosts two websites: www.milkweed.org, where readers can find in-depth information about Milkweed books, authors, and programs, and www.worldashome.org, which is your online resource of books, organizations, and writings exploring the ethical, esthetic, and cultural dimensions of our relationship to the natural world.

Since its genesis in 1979 as *Milkweed Chronicle,* hundreds of emerging writers have reached their readers through Milkweed. Thanks to the generosity of foundations and individuals like you, Milkweed Editions is able to continue its nonprofit mission of publishing books chosen on the basis of literary merit—of how they impact the human heart and spirit—rather than on how they impact the bottom line. That's a miracle our readers have made possible.

In addition to purchasing Milkweed books, you can join the growing community of Milkweed supporters. Individual contributions of any amount are both meaningful and welcome. Contact us for a Milkweed catalog or log on to www.milkweed.org and click on "About Milkweed," then "Why join Milkweed," to find out about our donor program, or simply call 800-520-6455 and ask about becoming one of Milkweed's contributors. As a nonprofit press, Milkweed belongs to you, the community. Milkweed's board, its staff, and especially the authors whose careers you help launch thank you for reading our books and supporting our mission in any way you can.

Interior design by Dale Cooney
Typeset in Sabon 11/15.5
by Stanton Publication Servies, Inc.
Printed on acid-free, recycled 55# Frasier Miami Book Natural paper
by Friesen Corporation